BONEYARD
NOSE ART

THE STACKPOLE MILITARY PHOTO SERIES

World War II

Blitzkrieg France 1940

First Winter on the Eastern Front

Operation Barbarossa 1941

Rommel's Desert Warriors

Steel Thunder on the Eastern Front

Vietnam

Bloody Jungle

Vietnam War Helicopter Art

BONEYARD NOSE ART

U.S. Military Aircraft Markings and Artwork

NICHOLAS A. VERONICO,
JIM DUNN, and RON STRONG

Foreword by John Brennan

STACKPOLE
BOOKS

Published by
STACKPOLE BOOKS
5067 Ritter Road
Mechanicsburg, PA 17055
www.stackpolebooks.com

10 9 8 7 6 5 4 3 2 1

Library of Congress Cataloging-in-Publication Data

Veronico, Nick, 1961–
    Boneyard nose art : U.S. military aircraft markings and artwork / Nicholas
A. Veronico, Jim Dunn, and Ron Strong ; foreword by John Brennan.
        pages cm. — (Stackpole photo series)
    Includes bibliographical references.
    ISBN 978-0-8117-1308-5
    1. Aerospace Maintenance and Regeneration Group (U.S.)—Pictorial works.
2. Airplanes, Military—United States—Markings.   3. Airplanes, Military—
United States—Pictorial works.   I. Dunn, Jim.   II. Strong, Ron.   III. Title.
    UG1243.V468 2013
    358.4'183—dc23
                                                        2013022262

CONTENTS

FOREWORD

William Faulkner once wrote, "The past is never dead. It's not even past." I love this quote because it speaks to the historian in me and it defines the heart of what the authors of *Boneyard Nose Art* aim to achieve with their book. It's something akin to being invited to a private, open-air art show, but with two differences: the art isn't for sale and the life of the art is terminal.

Simply put, military aircraft nose art in reality isn't meant to be seen by the public or to have a long life. Any acknowledgment of its existence today is the result of human intervention to preserve and document. Color photography has excelled at this, and *Boneyard Nose Art* relies on it to capture a miracle moment in the short lifespan of this colorful artwork. Like chalk art on a sidewalk or a scribbled line on a sandy beach, nothing can prevent its ill-fated end—except for a photograph to keep its visual memory alive.

The three authors have done a wonderful job of reminding readers of the rich heritage they have inherited. Among the detailed stories and photos is the tale of World War II's *Memphis Belle*: how the infamous bomber's name and bathing-suited beauty have been passed down through the generations to the combat aircraft of today. From my own Vietnam War research, I know that this name and art were affixed to at least two in-country U.S. Army helicopters in proud tribute to a legend.

Thank you, Nick Veronico, Jim Dunn, and Ron Strong, for helping save part of our aviation history.

John Brennan
Author of *Vietnam War Helicopter Art*

INTRODUCTION: ORIGINS AND EVOLUTION OF NOSE ART

Prior to the emergence of the aircraft and its introduction into a combat role in the early part of the twentieth century, the personalization of weapons was confined mostly to an elite class of warriors: the proven combatants who had earned the right to distinguish themselves from others on the battlefield. Standing out on the field of battle was meant to inspire pride and confidence among those who fought alongside those distinguished few and, at the same time, to instill fear and disorder in the enemy. Being seen on the battlefield by both friend and foe was as important then as *not* being seen is today.

Over time, how these individual warriors chose to identify themselves evolved much along the lines of the development of warfare and the equipment used to wage it, beginning with the application of a unique style of body art and then evolving into distinctive forms of attire from body armor to helmets. Others were to notice the warrior's presence on the battlefield and be heartened or intimidated by it. An army's

appearance was also used to control subjects in far-flung empires; subjugation required that the authority of the ruling power be respected, and the personification of that authority was the professional soldier.

For many centuries, a professional soldier could be distinguished by the horse that he rode. He was able to choose from the finest horses in the land and was given a support group to maintain and care for the animal. The combination of horse and rider was both a symbol of authority and a premier fighting unit. It would remain this way until the advent of modern warfare, when machines came to dominate the field of battle.

DISTINCTION IN AERIAL COMBAT

Early in the twentieth century, a new arena of warfare soon created another class of elite warriors. Less than three years after the Italians flew the first combat flights against Turkish positions in North Africa in October 1911, the use of airpower became a critical element in fighting the First World War.

Baron Manfred von Richtofen flew an Albatros D.III that he had painted bright red in January 1917. It was in the Albatros that Richtofen gained the name "Red Baron." He began flying the Fokker Dr.I triplane in July 1917 and scored nineteen of his eighty aerial victories in the type that is so closely associated with his name. The color of his aircraft built esprit de corps among his men and struck fear into his enemies.
VERONICO COLLECTION

Many of these early warplanes had difficulty simply getting into the air, and those that did had barely enough fabric covering on them to display national identity. This changed quickly with the rapid development of warplanes, and by 1917, aero squadrons and their ace pilots were the most publicized units of the war.

No unit or pilot would gain more fame than the German ace Baron Manfred von Richthofen and his "Flying Circus." Intent on striking fear into the enemy just by their presence in the air, the Flying Circus flew the most garishly colored aircraft ever to enter combat. Richthofen earned the nickname "The Red Baron" for his deadly skills while leading the Flying Circus in his blood-red Fokker Dr.I triplane. Before his death in combat on April 21, 1918, Richthofen was credited with eighty aerial victories.

By the end of the war, aircraft were emblazoned with national, unit, flight, and even personal names and markings. Some of the most colorful markings on Allied aircraft were those seen on French and American squadrons flying the Spad Scout. From the famous Sioux warrior of the Lafayette Escadrille, to the red, white, and blue "Hat in the Ring" of Capt. Eddie Rickenbacker's 94th Aero Squadron, the unit emblem was a proud form of identification. There was even a brief period after the war when many American Spads were decorated with a variety of very colorful individual paint schemes not unlike those of the "Flying Circus."

Between the world wars, a great deal of color could be seen on many United States Army Air Corps (USAAC), Navy, and Marine Corps aircraft. As tensions rose throughout the world in the late 1930s, different camouflage schemes began to appear. In a strange twist of fate, on September 1, 1939, just as Germany began its invasion of Poland, eighteen P-36Cs from the 27th Pursuit Squadron were performing at the National Air Races in Cleveland. Each of these fighters had been painted in a different water-based camouflage scheme just for this event. Although these somewhat bizarre-looking patterns were thought to be associated with the large war games that were taking place that year, these camouflage schemes were all part of the USAAC's experimentation to determine the best color pattern to enable the aircraft to blend into their backgrounds when seen from above or below.

NOSE ART AND THE *MEMPHIS BELLE*

History does not record the exact time or place of the first application of a cartoon figure or pinup girl on a warplane, but it clearly indicates that the biggest influence for its rapid spread came from a small group of American pilots fighting in the skies over China and Burma. The American Volunteer Group—the "Flying Tigers"—was one of the few success stories for the United States in the early days of World War II. The Flying Tigers displayed a fearsome shark mouth under the noses of their P-40s—a design that they had seen in an Indian magazine of Royal Air Force P-40s operating in North Africa—and soon images and tales of the American Volunteer Group's exploits against the Japanese became major news back home.

It was not long before groups of eager young airmen were being assigned the brand-new warplanes that American factories were building. Their enthusiasm to stand out and be recognized soon found a place on the noses of their aircraft. Nose art of all styles and sizes took off in 1942, and with the aid of the popular media, it was soon a big hit with warriors and civilians alike.

When it came to media coverage of the air campaigns, one aircraft caught the attention of the American people more than any other. Featured in newsreels since its first introduction in 1935, the Boeing B-17 Fly-

P-36Cs of the 27th Pursuit Squadron sit at the National Air Races in September 1939. Although these paint schemes were never worn in combat, camouflage patterns were still undergoing development in the years leading up to World War II. U.S. AIR FORCE

The Curtiss P-40s of the American Volunteer Group in China were some of the first U.S. military units to adorn their aircraft with nose art. The shark mouth is identified with the AVG and its follow-on unit, the 23rd Fighter Group. This example of a Curtiss P-40E is displayed at the National Museum of the U.S. Air Force in the colors of Col. Bruce Holloway, an AVG and 23rd Fighter Group pilot. NATIONAL MUSEUM OF THE U.S. AIR FORCE

The 91st Bomb Group's Boeing B-17F-10 *Memphis Belle* (41-24485) was the second Eighth Air Force bomber to complete twenty-five missions before rotating stateside. The plane's exploits were turned into a wartime movie directed by William Wyler. The bomber is seen over the English countryside preparing for its flight back to the United States. U.S. AIR FORCE

ing Fortress was a shining example of American ingenuity at the darkest point of the Great Depression. Now massive numbers of them were going to war, and the American people were interested in both their role in the fighting and the men who served in them.

The B-17 would be featured not only in newsreels, but also in major motion pictures such as the 1943 Howard Hawks classic *Air Force*, in which the B-17 *Mary Ann* was as much the star as any of the actors. This fictional story showing the attachment between a crew and its aircraft was followed that same year by the very

real story of another B-17 and the accomplishment of its historic crew.

Of the more than 12,700 B-17s built, one would become an American legend; for many, it is arguably the most famous aircraft to have fought in World War II. The legend began in early September 1942 at Dow Field in Bangor, Maine, when a brand-new B-17F—with United States Army Air Forces (USAAF) serial number 41-24485—was assigned to a young aircrew about to go overseas. By the end of that month, this B-17F would forever be known as the *Memphis Belle*.

Perhaps the most important factor in the proliferation of nose art on American aircraft in World War II was that the command structure for the most part adopted a hands-off policy on its application. Particularly within the USAAF, the practice of applying nose art to its aircraft was neither encouraged nor discouraged, and although it could be seen in all of the theaters of war, it would never become a practice accepted by everyone.

Once they had been assigned an aircraft of their own, an individual pilot or crew made the decision whether to name an aircraft or apply nose art. The privilege of getting one's own aircraft did not come quickly and sometimes never occurred at all. Pilots and crews assigned to training and ferry commands did not fly the same aircraft on a regular basis and often did not fly the same aircraft more than once. Pilots and crews who entered a squadron as replacements would most likely fly a number of missions in someone else's aircraft before being assigned one of their own.

Twenty-three year-old 2nd Lt. Robert Morgan from Asheville, North Carolina, was a newly trained B-17 pilot and, like his crew, was eager to get the journey to England underway to fulfill the role they had trained for. During his training, Morgan had witnessed the new practice of personalizing aircraft with a name and, more often than not, with some rather unique American form of artwork. Since the brass were not expressing any objections, Morgan was ready to join in when his B-17 arrived at Dow Field.

There was a special woman in Morgan's life whose name he wanted to paint on the side of his new aircraft, but the other nine crew members had their own thoughts on the matter. It would take some friendly persuasion by Morgan to make it happen.

For most of the crews, popular icons supplied the inspirational spark for the artwork being applied to these aircraft. Cartoon characters, movie stars, and especially pinup girls provided all the inspiration these young airmen could ask for, and in the case of Lieutenant Morgan, it would be a John Wayne film that solved his dilemma.

It was apparent to Morgan that his idea to name this B-17 after his girlfriend, Margaret Polk, was not going to fly with anyone else on the crew, but while watching the film *Lady for a Night*, something caught his eye. Featured in this film was a riverboat named the *Memphis Belle*, and it just so happened that Margaret Polk hailed from Memphis, Tennessee. Morgan soon convinced his crew to name their B-17 the *Memphis Belle*.

Now that the name had been chosen, it was time to find some special artwork to adorn the nose of the *Memphis Belle*.

Pinup art was at its zenith in the early 1940s, with alluring images of beautiful young females featured in dozens of catalogues, magazines, and calendars. In many instances, pinup art was an inexpensive form of merchandising that demonstrated that sex truly did sell, and in the years of the Great Depression, any medium that was this popular was going to be put to many different uses.

In Europe, the pinup was also popular, and several European magazines had introduced a new way to showcase it in their issues. The new style was known as a gatefold, offset double foldouts that would open to expose a glorious pinup inside. In December 1939, *Esquire* magazine introduced the gatefold to American audiences, and by April 1940, they were so popular that there were three in every issue.

Even before the gatefold, a highlight of each issue of *Esquire* was the "Petty Girl." Drawn by the magazine's top graphic artist, George Petty, the Petty Girl was one of America's favorite and most popular pinups. Now it was to *Esquire* and George Petty that Lieutenant Morgan turned in his quest to obtain the best pinup art available for the *Memphis Belle*.

Starting with a call to the New York offices of *Esquire*, Morgan began to tell his story. He convinced them to give him George Petty's phone number, and soon he was telling the story of the naming of the *Memphis Belle* to the artist. Petty grew enthusiastic about this project and promised Morgan to send him one of his Petty Girls for the *Memphis Belle*. Choosing an illustration from the April 1941 issue of *Esquire* that he thought would fit the name, he probably never dreamed of the fame that this Petty Girl would soon achieve.

With so many Americans now in uniform, it seemed like every squadron in the USAAF had an artist within their ranks. At Dow Field, assigned to the 91st Bomb Group, Cpl. Anthony "Tony" Starcer was a line mechanic whose unknown talent as an artist was just coming to light. After seeing some of his early works, Lieutenant Morgan knew that Corporal Starcer was the man to paint the *Memphis Belle*.

Handing over the artwork that he had received from George Petty, the only instructions that Morgan gave Starcer were to make sure that there was a bathing suit on her. Following these orders, Starcer added his own unique part to the history of the *Memphis Belle* by giving her a blue bathing suit on the left side of the nose and then painting her with a red bathing suit on the right side.

Memphis Belle's pilot, Capt. Robert Morgan, contacted George Petty, known for his "Petty Girls" in *Esquire*. Petty sent a pinup, titled *Telephone Girl*, which Cpl. Anthony "Tony" Starcer painted on both sides of the bomber's nose. Starcer added his own touch by painting the pinup with different colored swimsuits on each side of the aircraft. Starcer painted more than 120 nose art pieces. Here *Memphis Belle* is seen on display at Hartford, Connecticut, after its combat tour. U.S. AIR FORCE

Nose art can take on a life of its own. Considered "lucky," many World War II nose art went on to make appearances in later conflicts. *Memphis Belle II* was worn by an F-105 during the Vietnam War. F-105D 60-0504 was flown by Maj. Buddy Jones with the 357th Tactical Fighter Squadron (355th Tactical Fighter Wing) from Takhli Royal Thai Air Base and was credited with two aerial victories over MiG-17s. That aircraft is now on display at the National Museum of the United States Air Force in Dayton, Ohio. An FB-111 also wore the name *Memphis Belle II* and is now displayed at the Strategic Air Command Museum in Nebraska. TONY SACKETOS

The famous image of the *Memphis Belle* once again returned to combat when A-10A 80-0229—assigned to the 511th Tactical Fighter Squadron at RAF Alconbury, England—deployed to Saudi Arabia for Desert Shield and Desert Storm in 1990–91. Seen here in May 1992 at McClellan AFB awaiting depot-level maintenance, *Memphis Belle III* continues to serve today—without its name and nose art—with the 66th Weapons Squadron at Nellis AFB, Nevada.
JIM DUNN

A pair of Boeing B-52s have worn the *Memphis Belle* name, including Gulf War veterans B-52G 59-2954 *Memphis Belle III* and B-52H 60-0001 *Memphis Belle IV*. Other aircraft have worn the nose art: B-1B Lancer 86-0133 *Memphis Belle* and C-141 Starlifter 67-0024 *Memphis Belle V*. U.S. AIR FORCE

Tony Starcer would move with the *Memphis Belle* and the rest of the 91st Bomb Group to their wartime home in Bassingbourn, England. By the end of the war, Starcer was credited with painting nose art on 124 aircraft, including such well-known B-17s as *Nine O Nine*, *Out House Mouse*, and *Shoo Shoo Baby*. Like many, he would retire his wartime talent after going home, only to return to it later in life, even repainting the nose art of *Shoo Shoo Baby* during its restoration in the 1980s.

By changing just a few of the details, the story of the naming of the *Memphis Belle* could be told about thousands of American airmen and crews stationed throughout the world. Someone or something in the lives of these young men would be the spark that helped ignite their imagination and desire to personalize these machines of war. What was different about the *Memphis Belle* is that the story did not end there, but instead continued on to involve an entire nation.

In the dark, early days of the bombing campaign in Europe, there was very little for the USAAF to cheer about. The 91st Bomb Group and the *Memphis Belle* flew their first mission on November 7, 1942. By Christmas, after only a handful of missions, the 91st Bomb Group had lost twenty-nine of the thirty-six aircraft that they had flown to England back in October. They also had yet to fly a mission into Germany.

For the bomber crews of the Eighth Air Force, these losses continued month after month. Mission number nine on February 4, 1943, was the first one that would take Robert Morgan—now a captain—and his crew over Germany. Their chances of surviving another sixteen missions to reach the magic number of twenty-five and return home were bleak.

A huge investment in both men and aircraft had been made to support the strategy of daylight bombing, so there can be no doubt about how significant the achievement was when the *Memphis Belle* brought her crew back to Bassingbourn after its twenty-fifth mission on May 17, 1943. Americans knew how high the cost was in this effort, and they were ready to honor their new heroes. (On May 13, 1943, a 303rd Bomb Group B-17F named *Hell's Angels*, commanded by Capt. Ira Baldwin, was the first to complete twenty-five missions. While the crew was rotated home, *Hell's Angels* continued to be flown on combat missions for several more months before returning for a morale-boosting and war bond–selling tour of stateside factories.)

For many Americans, this accomplishment became even more memorable because the *Memphis Belle* and her crew were already known to them. Shortly after the nose art had been painted, Morgan took the B-17 on an unscheduled flight to Memphis for Margaret Polk to christen her namesake. Newspapers there had picked up on this love story, and with the name and colorful illustration on this B-17, they spread it across the nation. The USAAF couldn't have orchestrated a better public-relations campaign.

After completing their missions, the *Memphis Belle* and her crew were sent home to begin a nationwide public-relations tour of thirty-three cities that lasted from June through August 1943. Along with all of the newspaper, newsreel, and magazine coverage, this tour helped to secure a place for both the *Memphis Belle* and nose art in the American psyche.

Despite all of the publicity—including an Academy Award–winning documentary released in 1944—the *Memphis Belle* was nearly lost to history when the war ended. After a tour in Florida training new bomber crews, the historic B-17 was sent to Altus, Oklahoma, for storage. Here thousands of war-weary aircraft were parked next to shiny new ones awaiting their fate. If not for one very determined person, the *Memphis Belle* would have been scrapped.

Walter Chandler, the mayor of Memphis, obtained the bomber from the Reconstruction Finance Corporation for $350. After decades of highs and lows on display in Memphis, the National Museum of the United States Air Force moved the aircraft to Dayton, Ohio, for a major restoration in 2005. When completed, it will be given a place of honor in this world-famous museum.

Without the famous name and nose art given to this B-17, how would history have recorded these events? Would a headline reading, "Crew of B-17 '485 First to Complete 25 Missions" have held the nation's attention for more than a day or two? Without the name and art to bestow a unique identity, it is almost certain that B-17F 41-24485 would have fallen victim to the scrap man just like nearly every other B-17 that came home from combat. There would have been nothing but a number to separate it from all of the others waiting to be destroyed.

Today, however, we have the *Memphis Belle* to remember the achievements of those men who flew her through those deadly skies. That name and its accompanying nose art still capture our collective imagination.

Halfway around the globe, other artists were decorating aircraft, including the 20th Combat Mapping Squadron's Al Merkling, who painted *Patched Up Piece* on photo-reconnaissance B-24 (F-7A) 42-64047. Some of Merkling's other paintings include *Photo Queen*, *The Wango Wango Bird*, and the C-47 *Hot Pants*. VERONICO COLLECTION

Artist Gil Elvgren's pinup *Sport Model* appeared in a number of products, from magazines to cards sold out of Mutoscope vending machines. *Sport Model* was faithfully reproduced on VPB-106 PB4Y-2 59370 *Joy Rider* (a play on aircraft commander Lt. Bernard F. Joy Jr.'s last name. VERONICO COLLECTION / DAVE BARMORE

San Diego–built Consolidated B-24D-160 42-72829 served with the Thirteenth Air Force's 5th Bomb Group, 394th Bomb Squadron, flying out of the Philippines during World War II. The pinup for *Hell from Heaven* was inspired by an Alberto Vargas drawing. JIM HAWKINS COLLECTION

Nose art on PB4Y-1 *Chick's Chick*, flown by John T. "Chick" Hayward, commander of Patrol Squadron 106 (VPB-106). After combat duties, Hayward worked on the Manhattan Project to develop the atomic bomb. He would later rise to the rank of admiral and be instrumental in the Navy's development of nuclear-powered surface ships as well as ground- and air-launched missiles. JIM HAWKINS COLLECTION

Slugger Sue was a Consolidated B-24D built at the company's San Diego factory. Assigned Army Air Forces serial number 42-41215, the bomber served with the Thirteenth Air Force's 424th Bomb Squadron of the 307th Bomb Group. JIM HAWKINS COLLECTION

The Navy's version of the Liberator bomber was the Consolidated PB4Y-2 Privateer. This aircraft featured non-supercharged engines for better low-altitude performance, power turrets in every gun position, and an extended fuselage to accommodate a radar operator and a second top turret. The extended fuselage made for a great nose-art canvas, as can be seen on Navy Bureau of Aeronautics serial number 59491, known as *Tail Chaser*, which served in the Pacific theater with distinction. JIM SULLIVAN COLLECTION VIA RON SATHRE

General Motors FM-2 Wildcat *Smokey's Lucky Witch* wears multiple pieces of nose art. To the right is the popular Alberto Vargas *Sleepy Time Gal* pinup from *Esquire*. The pilot is Ens. Darrell C. Bennett (USNR), seen aboard the escort carrier USS *Gambier Bay* (CVE-73) on August 1, 1944. This carrier was sunk on October 25, 1944, off Samar Island, Philippines, by Japanese naval gunfire—the only carrier sunk by gunfire in World War II. NATIONAL ARCHIVES

One of the largest and best pieces of nose art from World War II was the Fifth Air Force's San Diego–built B-24J 44-49073 *The Dragon and His Tail*, flown with the 43rd Bomb Group's 64th Bomb Squadron. The dragon's tail stretched all the way back to the tail turret. Considered an aviation art masterpiece, it was painted by Staff Sgt. Sarkis E. Bartigian of Chelsea, Massachusetts, a talented artist and graduate of the Rhode Island School of Design. Bartigian also painted *Cocktail Hour, It Ain't So Funny, Mabel's Labels,* and *Michigan.* After the war, *The Dragon and His Tail* returned stateside for storage and final disposition at Kingman, Arizona. The workers there wanted to see the bomber saved and kept moving it around the airfield among more than 5,400 aircraft. They were successful in delaying the bomber's fate: it was the last plane to be scrapped in 1948. ROBERT KROPP COLLECTION

The Dragon and His Tail nose art lived on to adorn the fuselage of The Collings Foundation's restored ex-RAF and former Indian Air Force B-24J 44-44052, which was built at Consolidated's Fort Worth, Texas, assembly plant in August 1944. The foundation barnstorms its collection of historic aircraft around the United States to more than 120 cities each year and paints its Liberator to honor various veteran groups. From 1998 to 2005, the B-24J wore *The Dragon and His Tail* nose art in tribute to all of the Liberator veterans of the Pacific War. In 2005, it was repainted as the 467th Bomb Group's *Witchcraft.* NICHOLAS A. VERONICO

MORE NOSE ART

The popularity of nose art was not confined to bomber crews in the European theater, nor was it exclusive to the U.S. Army Air Forces. Navy and Marine Corps squadrons in the Pacific were also very proud of their nose art, with shore-based units in particular sporting some large and colorful nose art. This was especially true among patrol-bomber and night-fighter squadrons. One Marine Corps night-fighter squadron, the "Bateyes" of VMF(N)-541, had their F6F-5N Hellcats decorated with some of the best pinup nose art of any sccn in the war.

Nose art would nearly vanish when the fighting in the Pacific came to an end with the dropping of two atomic bombs on Japan. What was once a great morale booster for many in and out of uniform during the war could now only be found fading away on the sides of aircraft in boneyards around the country. Many considered it folk art, another wartime fad that had run its course.

Plans were well underway for the new postwar professional military that would represent and defend America's position in the world. The USAAF's goal to separate itself from the U.S. Army and become its own separate branch, the U.S. Air Force, was about to be realized, and the professionalism of the newly independent branch would leave few places for the wartime fad.

In the brief stretch of time between World War II and the Korean War, not only was the U.S. Air Force established (on September 1, 1947), but jet aircraft were introduced, and the Cold War with the Soviet Union began. These events led to significant changes in the operational structure of the new USAF. During this period, nose art all but disappeared, with most of what remained being found in fighter squadrons based in Europe and Japan. Rank hath its privileges, and art was often found on aircraft assigned to squadron commanders.

Painting names on aircraft noses was a more common practice, but that, too, was not widespread in this period. One small enclave where both names and nose art lived on was in the flight-test community. Out in the high desert of California at Muroc Air Force Base (renamed Edwards AFB in 1949), no one was going to make a fuss, considering the risk that these crews were taking while performing their missions.

Squadron colors and unit emblems on aircraft made a return at this time. This was especially true in the fighter squadrons of the newly created Air National Guard (ANG). Manned by some of the most experienced World War II pilots, these squadrons were known derisively as "ANG Flying Clubs" by senior USAF leadership. Coming under the authority of the state to which they were assigned, these squadrons were much more freewheeling than their active-duty counterparts, and it often showed on their aircraft.

Over in the Navy and Marine Corps, the postwar years would be rather colorless. For the most part, aircraft were painted in standard glossy sea blue and devoid of most squadron colors and emblems, although many Marine Corps aircraft after the war would carry the Marine Corps emblem on their nose. Very few, if any, personal markings were seen in this period. It would take another major conflict before change came about.

NOSE ART IN THE KOREAN AND VIETNAM WARS

Major conflict erupted on the Korean Peninsula on June 25, 1950, when North Korea invaded the American-allied nation of South Korea. Over the next few months, many of the USAF Reserve, Air National Guard, Naval Reserve, and Marine Corps Reserve squadrons were called to active duty. In addition, tens of thousands of World War II–veteran aircrew would be recalled to active service. With them came some familiar traditions from the last war.

Among these traditions were naming an aircraft and giving it some nose art. Many World War II veterans gave their new aircraft the same name as the one they flew in the previous war, often just adding Roman numerals to the end of the name to designate its lineage. In some cases, the veterans of World War II included aircraft—for example, the B-29 *Snuggle Bunny*, which would add seventy-five combat missions over Korea to the sixty-five that it had completed in World War II.

While nose art may not have been used as widely during the Korean War as in World War II, there were still some eye-catching applications to be seen. The largest examples, at least in terms of actual size, could be found in several squadrons operating the Fairchild C-119 Flying Boxcar. Just entering widespread service, this slab-sided, twin-engine giant presented its crews and squadron artists with a great opportunity to express themselves. Their pinup-girl creations were big and colorful and would never again be seen at that size on U.S. military aircraft.

What did make a widespread and more lasting return during the Korean War was the use of color to identify individual squadrons within a larger organization. This had the dual benefit of helping to determine which squadron was which during flight operations

Nose art continued into the Korean War. *The Outlaw* was painted in tribute to actress Jane Russell and her appearance in the 1941 film of the same name, which was quite risqué for the time, with producer Howard Hughes reportedly designing a special brassiere to enhance Russell's already ample breasts. The aircraft, a B-29 built by Martin Aircraft in Omaha, Nebraska, with serial number 42-65306, served with the 28th Bomb Squadron, 19th Bomb Group, based at Kadena AFB, Okinawa, Japan. This aircraft participated in the first Air Force mission of the Korean War and later crashed on takeoff at Kadena after losing its number-one engine as the bomber lifted from the runway on October 2, 1951. RENÉ FRANCILLON COLLECTION

and on the airfields and flight decks and of promoting unit pride and cohesion. In a way, this enhanced esprit de corps lessened the desire for nose art since an individual could now point out his unit's aircraft more clearly.

After the signing of the Korean Armistice on July 27, 1953, the USAF returned to a more toned-down peacetime standard. Within the United States, the most colorful aircraft were to be found in Air Defense Command (ADC) and ANG squadrons, while in Europe the fighters assigned to wing commanders took on a rainbow of color as they wore a different color stripe for each squadron in the wing.

Over in the bomber community, the introduction of the B-52 Stratofortress to operational service in the Strategic Air Command (SAC) continued a tradition of applying large unit emblems on both sides of the nose. Beginning with the B-36, these colorful emblems would represent either SAC or the wing to which the bomber was assigned. Most B-36s and early-model B-52s carried these emblems all the way to their final end in the boneyard at Davis-Monthan AFB in Tucson, Arizona.

A major change for Navy and USMC aircraft began in 1955 with the adoption of a new overall paint scheme. The change from the standard glossy sea blue

The dragon-and-his-tail motif lived on in Korea as well. Built at Boeing's factory in Renton, Washington, B-29A 44-62253 was delivered too late to see combat during World War II. It was called up for service in Korea with the 345th Bomb Squadron, 98th Bomb Group, flying missions from Yokota, Japan, and is seen in late 1951. After the war, it was sent to Davis-Monthan AFB for storage. The war-weary bomber was scrapped on July 14, 1954.
EARL HOLMQUIST

to a light gull grey, with insignia white under surfaces, ushered in an era that would continue through both war and peace for nearly thirty years.

Color ruled the day during this period. Squadrons had their colors, and many units applied colorful reproductions of their logos to the aircraft. In some squadrons, the entire tail of the aircraft was dominated by logos that depicted everything from the bright green "Shamrocks" of VS-41 to the brilliant red sunset of the "Sundowners" of VF-111.

In aviation squadrons assigned aboard aircraft carriers, each squadron designates one aircraft for the use of the commander of the carrier air group (CAG). Known as "CAG birds," these aircraft carry the colors of all of the squadrons on their tails, a tradition that produced some of the most colorful aircraft markings

in U.S. military history. Even at the height of the Vietnam War, these Navy squadrons retained all of their brightly colored markings.

It was carrier-based Navy aircraft that made the first air strike on North Vietnam on August 5, 1964, in response to an attack on American destroyers in the Gulf of Tonkin. Nine years later, a B-52 strike on Cambodia finally ended this costly air campaign. What took place during this period was profoundly different from any other past U.S. military action, and its effects on the services were to be long-lasting.

The USAF already had a long involvement in Southeast Asian air operations prior to its first combat strike on North Vietnam on February 8, 1965. There were still some World War II and Korean War veterans—Chuck Yeager, Bud Anderson, and Robin Olds

During the Vietnam War, nose art was limited to names rather than pinups. Here Wichita-built B-52D-25 55-0677 wears the name *City of Fort Worth*. It was based with the 7th Bomb Wing at nearby Carswell AFB. This B-52D is seen on the ramp at Kelly AFB, outside San Antonio, Texas. It was eventually retired to the boneyard on September 12, 1983, and was scrapped in the late 1990s. TERRY PANOPALIS

among them—who flew combat missions in this war, but there would be no large-scale call-up of ANG squadrons to rush in to support operations.

For the USAF, aircraft markings underwent a radical change. Gone forever were the flashy silver finishes of the 1950s, now replaced with dull green/brown camouflage schemes. Gone as well in the combat zone were squadron colors, now replaced by two-digit alpha tail codes. The only colors left were on U.S.-based ANG fighters and fighter interceptors assigned to Air Defense Command (ADC).

In Southeast Asia, nose art made a very limited return, and its style and application were much cruder than in previous times. For the most part, pinup girls were no longer the beautiful creations of talented artists, but instead were often distorted and sometimes vulgar. This style, however, did seem to match the mood of the times.

Nose art was seen mostly in squadrons flying the Republic F-105 Thunderchief. Known as the "Thud," this large, single-engine tactical fighter-bomber was the workhorse of the war. Based in Thailand, F-105 squadrons

Boeing's eight-engine B-52D Stratofortresses were the mainstay of the bombing campaign in Vietnam. B-52D-80 56-0618 was built at Boeing's Seattle factory and flew its missions over Vietnam from Andersen AFB in Guam. It is seen at Kelly AFB in May 1967 wearing 30 bomb mission symbols. It was last flown by the 22nd Bombardment Wing (Heavy) at March AFB in California and was flown to storage on November 30, 1978. TERRY PANOPALIS

were tasked with carrying the war to the North Vietnamese, and they would pay a very high price.

The Thud seemed the perfect aircraft for a name and nose art, although this time they were painted in places other than the nose. Names were often painted on the prominent air intakes that jutted from the wings, while nose art was mostly to be found near the bomb bay. Later in the war, two-seat Thuds assigned the deadly Wild Weasel mission appeared with large fearsome shark mouths on their noses, reminiscent of the famous P-40 Flying Tiger squadrons of World War II.

One example of Thud nose art will be remembered as one of the most bawdy ever seen on a U.S. military aircraft. Only a select group of aircrew could actually view it, however. Wanting to provide a little amusement to tanker crews doing air-to-air refueling, Capt. Vic Viscarra painted a very full-figured nude strategically placed to straddle the refueling receptacle on the top of the two F-105Ds that he flew during his tour. Named *Pussy Galore* and *Pussy Galore II*, these Thuds would never be forgotten by those few who saw them up close from the belly of a KC-135 over a hostile country.

Awaiting their fates in the boneyard on the backside of McClellan AFB, F-4C 63-7442 *Baby* and F-4C 63-7618 were two of the three F-4Cs from the 171st FIS that were flown to McClellan for disposal. The third Phantom, F-4C 64-0706, would find a permanent home in the Aerospace Museum of California at McClellan Field in Sacramento. In the background, crews from the 2951st Aircraft Battle Damage and Repair (ABDR) Squadron remove the fuselage of an F-105 that had served its final duty at the base. JIM DUNN

Another Phantom sent to the boneyard at McClellan AFB was F-4C 63-7649 *Nene* from the 199th Tactical Fighter Squadron of the Hawaii ANG at Hickam AFB. Early results of damage inflicted by the 2951st ABDR Squadron can be seen on the left intake of the aircraft. The Hawaii ANG often gives traditional Hawaiian names to their aircraft. JIM DUNN

What better aircraft to return the fearsome shark mouth to combat than the Republic F-105 Thunderchief. During the Vietnam War, several units flying the Wild Weasel mission from bases in Thailand carried shark mouths on their F-105F/Gs deep into North Vietnam to attack surface-to-air missile sites. After the war, the 128th Tactical Fighter Squadron of the Georgia ANG retained the design on the noses of its F-105F/Gs. One of the squadron's former aircraft, probably a F-105F, leaves the boneyard at McClellan AFB, California, in July 1986 for its final journey to the scrapper. JIM DUNN

COLD WAR COMEBACK

When the long conflict in Southeast Asia finally ended, just about the only artwork that came home were the shark mouths on the F-105 Wild Weasels. This dull post-Vietnam era would soon become the even more colorless age of tactical paint schemes and low-visibility markings; color was seen as an enemy. It was to get even worse when the dark world of stealth technology arrived, and the only color that mattered was black.

There was, however, one unit in the early 1980s that unknowingly started a renaissance period for nose art that continues to this day. Based at Plattsburgh AFB in New York, the 380th Bomb Wing was one of two SAC units assigned the General Dynamics FB-111A. After an experiment using nose art to boost esprit de corps, the commander authorized some additional nose art for an upcoming 380th Bomb Wing reunion. In World War II, the 380th Bomb Wing had flown B-24s over Europe, and to honor this service, FB-111A 69-6510 was given a very faithful reproduction of the nose art that was carried by the B-24 *Sleepy Time Gal*. What followed brought nose art back from the brink of extinction.

Special markings had often been allowed during military competitions. For an upcoming SAC bombing competition, the 380th Bomb Wing dispatched *Sleepy Time Gal* and another aircraft, named *Lucky Strike*. With these classic examples of World War II pinup-girl nose art on their sides, they introduced this old tradition to a whole new generation of American aircrew. Since this art paid tribute to the unit's heritage at a time when President Ronald Reagan was restoring pride in military service, it was seen as an appropriate way to demonstrate unit pride.

Wearing what remains of its markings from its participation in the William Tell Weapons Meet in 1978 and 1980, this McDonnell F-101B Voodoo from the 111th FIS of the Texas ANG is headed for the scrapper after the 2951st ABDR Squadron at McClellan AFB had completed its training on it. This training would pay dividends a few years later when the squadron put its skills to work returning battle-damaged A-10s to combat during Operation Desert Storm. JIM DUNN

The revival took hold when the 509th Bomb Wing, the only other operators of the FB-111A, began to apply nose art from their past to the nose gear doors of their aircraft. Soon other bomber units in SAC flying the B-1 and B-52 started to add nose art, as did the tanker units operating the KC-10 and KC-135. Tail art also began to appear on some of the black aircraft in SAC, such as the U-2 and SR-71. By the end of the 1980s, nose art was well established in SAC and was gaining a foothold elsewhere when another conflict developed that would assure its return as a wartime tradition.

That conflict would be short and intense, with air power playing the dominant role and taking center stage in the media's coverage of the operation. The First Gulf War—Operations Desert Shield and Desert Storm—began with the Iraqi invasion of Kuwait on August 2, 1990. It concluded with a ceasefire on February 28, 1991, after only a four-day ground campaign that had been preceded by devastating air attacks (starting on January 17, 1991).

A wave of patriotism swept the nation during the Gulf War, matched by high morale within the military. For the first time since the end of World War II, a victory was openly celebrated, and those who served were treated as heroes. As the aircraft that had fought the war returned home, many had their first opportunity to view nose art and mission markings up close. They

When the 2951st was finished with F-101B 57-0393, several McDonnell F-4Cs arrived at McClellan AFB to present a more current airframe on which to perform the battle-damage training. Among those F-4Cs were 63-0432 from the 196th TFS of the California ANG and 63-7442 from the 171st FIS of the Michigan ANG. JIM DUNN

were a big hit, and more importantly, they were once again looked on as an accepted tradition of aircrew during a period of war.

Following the First Gulf War, the 1992 merger of SAC and Tactical Air Command to create Air Combat Command (ACC) set the tone for the current state of nose art and other markings. Today in ACC, the bomber community continues to display nose art on its B-1s and B-52s, while each B-2 Spirit stealth bomber carries the name of a state on its main gear doors. In other USAF commands—the KC-135 tanker force, for example—nose art is still strong, and the A-10 carries on the tradition of the P-40 with shark mouth and fearsome tusks painted on its nose.

Nose art never became widespread in Navy and Marine Corps squadrons after World War II. In these units, it was squadron identification that always seemed to be placed above all else. Over the last few years, naval aviation has been able to celebrate the return of CAG birds to the squadrons, bringing all of their colors and unit symbols back into a world of tactical grey. This came just in time to mark the one hundredth anniversary of naval aviation in 2011, when a series of aircraft were repainted to commemorate and honor the great events and achievements of those who have served.

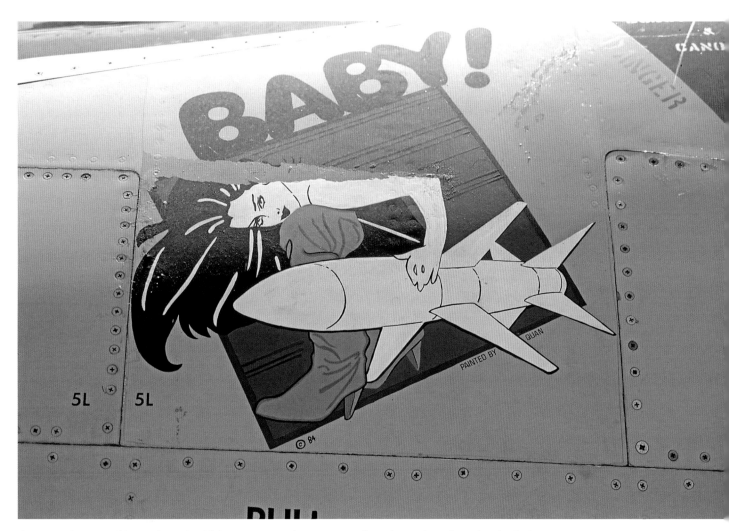

On occasion, a military aircraft will be sent to retirement at a location other than AMARG. Some aircraft are kept at their final duty stations as museum or gate-guard displays, or they end up in the base burn pit for use in training firefighting personnel. A few are sent to other bases to spend their final service being destroyed for training purposes. Assigned to the 171st Fighter Interceptor Squadron of the Michigan ANG, F-4C 63-7442 was given the name *Baby* during the unit's participation in the 1984 William Tell Weapons Meet at Tyndall AFB in Florida. In July 1986, it was retired to McClellan AFB for use by the 2951st ABDR Squadron. Aircraft used for these purposes are soon stricken from the inventory and later sold for scrap. JIM DUNN

These two classic re-creations of nose art first painted on a pair of B-24s during World War II would be a major factor in the resurgence of nose art in the 1980s USAF. The commander of the 380th Bomb Wing at Plattsburgh AFB allowed *Sleepy Time Gal* to be applied to FB-111A 69-6510 and *Lucky Strike* to FB-111A 68-0244. Other units in the Strategic Air Command followed suit. Soon nose art could be found throughout the USAF when it returned to combat during Operations Desert Shield and Desert Storm. KARL KORNCHUK / JIM DUNN

B-52G 58-0236 wore the name *Lucky 13*, accompanied by a black cat walking under a ladder—all superstitious signs representing bad luck. After the Gulf War, *Lucky 13* was flown by the 2nd Bomb Wing at Barksdale AFB in Louisiana and was fittingly retired to the boneyard on October 13, 1992. The bomber was eliminated under the Strategic Arms Reduction Treaty on April 29, 1999. RON STRONG

There are some aircraft, such as the famous Lockheed SR-71 Blackbird, whose design makes the application of traditional nose art impractical. This would not stop SR-71 crews from participating in the return of artwork on USAF aircraft back in the 1980s. The large vertical tail of the Blackbird presented the opportunity to carry artwork without compromising the highly secret missions flown by the spyplane. Assigned to the 9th Strategic Reconnaissance Wing at Beale AFB in California, SR-71A 64-17960 is seen on March 24, 1998, making an approach to nearby McClellan AFB adorned with the marking best described as *Great White Shark II*. JIM DUNN

POLITICAL CORRECTNESS IN THE NEW MILLENNIUM

Unfortunately, with only very few exceptions, nose art featuring a pinup girl is no longer viewed as appropriate on U.S. military aircraft. The current USAF regulation (Air Mobility Command Instruction 21-105, Aircraft Markings and Insignia, dated March 11, 2004) that squadron commanders must follow when considering a request for the application of nose art on one of their aircraft dictates:

4.2.1. Nose art is authorized on one aircraft per flying squadron, plus the wing pride aircraft. Additionally, one aircraft per wing may have the "Let's Roll" graphic applied as nose art; it may be on one of the above aircraft, or in addition to the above aircraft. Nose art is not permitted on any aircraft flying missions where local populations may consider it sensitive or offensive. Art will reflect a theme of civic and community pride, be distinctive, symbolic, and designed and maintained to the highest quality standards. Positioning of nose art is at the discretion of the wing commander; however, it must be forward of the wing leading edge and not interfere with any mandatory markings. Nose art should be approximately two-thirds the size of the fuselage national star insignia, not to exceed three feet in diameter. All nose art applied to wing aircraft will be of standard size and location. Nose art and tail flash designs must be approved prior to installation; . . . AMC-gained AFRC units will comply with HQ AFRC nose art guidance.

And with that guidance, the pinup girl went by the wayside. Patriotic, commemorative, and civic-related themes now dominate the noses of military aircraft, but that's not a bad thing. Many of today's nose art paintings are mini-murals, highly detailed and exquisitely decorated.

Every visit to AMARG is different. Here C-130s of various models and configurations sit where more than 800 F-4 Phantoms used to roost. F-14s, F-15s, and F-16s all occupied this space at one time or another, and before that, it was B-47 Stratojets and KC-97 Stratotankers. AMARG got its start after World War II as a strategic reserve holding B-29 Superfortress bombers and C-47 Skytrain transports. NICHOLAS A. VERONICO

In the second decade of the twenty-first century, many military planes are being phased out of service for a variety of reasons, many because of age. America's military aircraft storage center is known as AMARG, an acronym for the 309th Aerospace Maintenance and Regeneration Group, adjacent to Davis-Monthan AFB outside Tucson, Arizona.* The group operates as part of the Air Force Material Command and is home to more than 4,400 aircraft belonging to all branches of the U.S. military (Army, Air Force, Marine Corps, and Navy), as well as other Department of Defense customers and federal agencies, such as NASA, the Forestry Service, and the Department of Homeland Security.

Many of the aircraft stored at AMARG are adorned with nose art or other unusual markings. Some can be seen on the public tours operated by the Pima Air & Space Museum, and others will stay tucked away on the backfields of AMARG. As a course of normal business, AMARG reparks older tenant aircraft and positions new arrivals in a variety of locations as they go through the intake process. Thus, every visit to the military's aircraft boneyard is different, and what the camera captures on one visit may not be able to be seen on the next.

---

*Although AMARG has been known by a variety of different names and acronyms over the years, we have chosen to use the facility's current designation to avoid confusion among MASDC, AMARC, and AMARG. We also use Davis-Monthan interchangeably with AMARG.

CHAPTER 1
FIGHTER NOSE ART AND MARKINGS

Fighter and reconnaissance model F-4 Phantom IIs await an uncertain fate at AMARG. Some will become drones while others will yield parts to keep the flying targets in the air. Phantoms featured some interesting markings and their slab sides made for great canvases. NICHOLAS A. VERONICO

1

The twenty-first aircraft on the Fiscal Year 1980 USAF order was F-15C 80-021, which was first assigned to the 525th Tactical Fighter Squadron of the 36th Tactical Fighter Wing at Bitburg Air Base in West Germany. This Eagle would gain the name of *Black Jack* while flown by its final unit, the 114th Fighter Squadron of the Oregon ANG, based at Klamath Falls. On November 2, 2007, a Missouri ANG F-15C came apart in flight, leading to a grounding and inspection of all U.S. Air Force Eagles. Several aircraft were found to have structural problems in their upper longerons, including four Eagles from the 114th. *Black Jack* was one of those Eagles, and its career ended on July 31, 2008, when it was retired to AMARG. JIM DUNN

The nose art and name *Gulf Spirit* is carried on this jet of the 33rd Fighter Wing and its largest organization, the 33rd Operations Group. Based at Eglin AFB, Florida, and known as the Nomads, the 33rd transitioned from the F-15 to the F-35 in September 2009, with the 33rd Operations Group becoming the F-35 training unit for all Air Force, Navy, Marine, and international pilots on this new aircraft. Retired to AMARG on September 8, 2009, F-15C 83-0030 *Gulf Spirit* was a combat veteran of the First Gulf War, when it deployed to Dhahran, Saudi Arabia, during its previous assignment with the 27th Tactical Fighter Squadron of the 1st Tactical Fighter Wing based at Langley AFB. RON STRONG / JIM DUNN

During Operation Desert Storm, Maj. Jim Rose of the 706th Tactical Fighter Squadron racked up an impressive score card with his A-10A 77-0273 *Desert Rose.* His tally included fourteen tanks, sixteen artillery pieces, and sixteen trucks, along with a Scud launcher and eight radar sites. The artwork was applied by T/Sgt. George Cunnikin Jr., who painted several other A-10As from the 706th. *Desert Rose* was retired on October 22, 1992, with 3,653.3 hours of flight time. NICHOLAS A. VERONICO / JIM DUNN

The 706th Tactical Fighter Squadron was the only Air Force Reserve fighter squadron to be called to active duty for the Gulf War. It would go on to write a proud history by becoming the A-10A unit to score the most kills during Desert Storm. Since New Orleans is known as the Cresent City, it is appropriate that the artwork for A-10A 77-0269 *Belle of New Orleans* displays a belle reclining on a crescent moon. This Thunderbolt ended its flying days on July 27, 1992, with 3,085.7 hours in its logbook. JIM DUNN

Flown by Maj. Richard Sachitano, A-10A 77-0272 *Operation Desert Storm* was one of several A-10As from the 706th Tactical Fighter Squadron that were also forward-deployed to a small civilian airfield named Al Jouf in the northwestern area of Saudi Arabia. Tours at Al Jouf would last up to five days, with two Thunderbolts kept on standby alert to perform search-and-rescue missions. *Operation Desert Storm* was sent into retirement on July 13, 1992, with a total of 3,508.4 hours of flight time. JIM DUNN

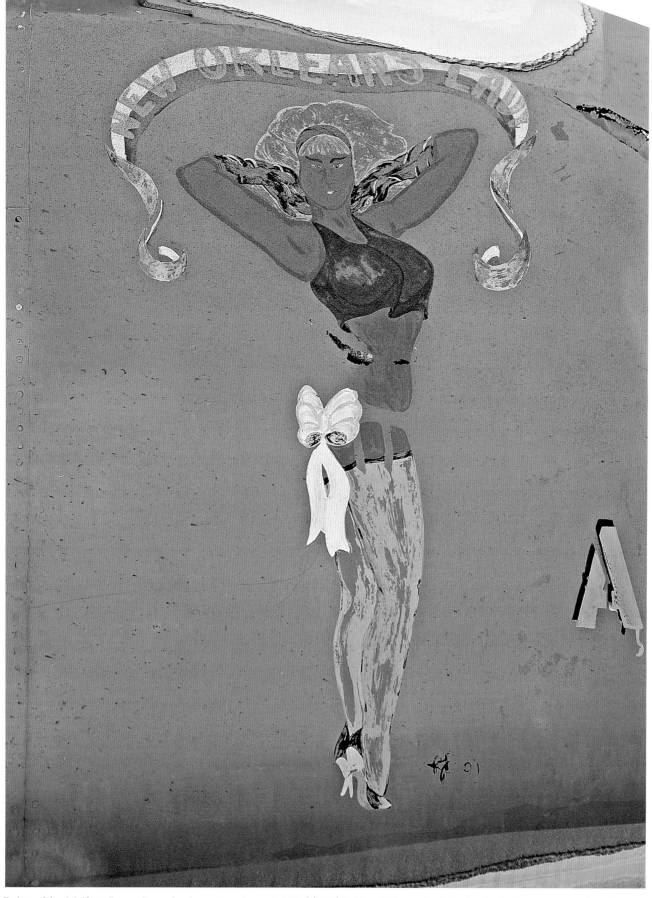

Painted by M/Sgt. Perry Bonck, the artwork on A-10A 77-0274 *New Orleans Lady* is slowly fading away under the blazing Tucson sun. Flown by Maj. Richard Pauly, it scored kills on seven tanks, four armored vehicles, seven artillery pieces, three radar sites, and eight trucks. After the 706th Tactical Fighter Squadron retired its Thunderbolts in 1992, the unit flew F-16s for four years before returning to the A-10A in 1996. In 2006, the renamed 706th Fighter Squadron relocated from NAS New Orleans to Nellis AFB, Nevada, where it flies a variety of fighter aircraft. *New Orleans Lady* had 3,631.5 hours on it when retired on October 5, 1992. JIM DUNN

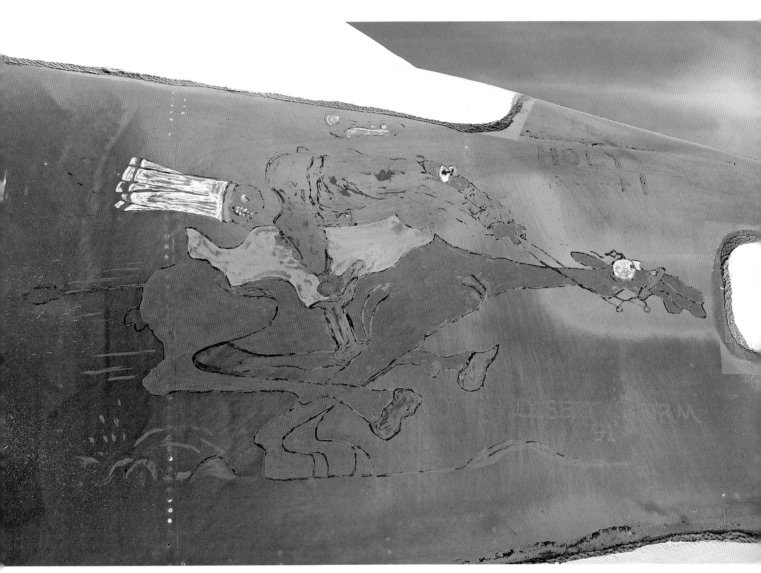

The final remaining nose art at AMARG that had been applied in a theater of combat can be found on a few A-10A Thunderbolts from the 706th Tactical Fighter Squadron. Based at NAS New Orleans, the 706th was deployed to King Fahd Airport, Saudi Arabia, in January 1991, in support of Operation Desert Shield. Credited with the destruction of four Scud missile launchers during the conflict, A-10A 77-0271 *Holy *~...+!* was flown into retirement on August 17, 1992, with 3,383.9 hours on its airframe. JIM DUNN

The initial production order for Fairchild A-10 Thunderbolt II attack aircraft was delivered in the 1970s. Its 30mm GAU-8 cannon made it lethal to tanks and other ground targets. In the early 2000s, the Air Force contracted with Lockheed Martin Systems Integration to provide upgrade kits for more than 350 aircraft, which would be added to the service life extension program (SLEP) underway at the Air Force Material Command's Ogden Air Logistics Center at Hill AFB, Utah, and at AMARG. Here aircraft were given new wings, extending the A-10's service life to the year 2040. The upgrade also converts the aircraft to a glass cockpit with a pair of 5x5-inch multifunction displays instead of the analog instruments, enables the aircraft to deploy "smart" weapons, and gives it enhanced electronic countermeasures capabilities. Aircraft that undergo this conversion are redesignated as C models. A-10A 79-0106 flew with the 356th Fighter Squadron of the 354th Tactical Fighter Wing before going into storage at AMARG. After the SLEP, the aircraft flew with the 47th Fighter Squadron, 917th Wing (Barksdale AFB), and wore the names *Tigress* and *High Maintenance*. A-10C 79-0106 is seen at AMARG in March 2010, before the attack fighter went overseas to the Far East. It was seen at Yokota, Japan, and Osan, Korea, in 2011. NICHOLAS A. VERONICO

56-0467 to set a world speed record of 1,525.95 mph on December 15, 1959, which is noted on the left rear of the plane. Subsequent to its retirement in 1988, 59-0043 went to the F-106 drone program, hence the high-visibility drone markings. The photo with the all-orange tail shows the Delta Dart after its return from flying the drone program with the 475th Weapons Evaluation Group at Tyndall AFB. This QF-106 has been parked at AMARG since March 4, 1998. ARMAND H. VERONICO / KAREN VERONICO / NICHOLAS A. VERONICO

NASA used this F-106B with serial number 59-0130 for its Eclipse Project to demonstrate the towed-launch vehicle concept. C-141A (serial number 61-2775) towed the F-106 aloft. This combination was used to determine if a space vehicle could be towed to 40,000 feet and subsequently launched into orbit. Tow launching enables a greater payload versus a vertical, rocket-boosted launch from the ground. The Eclipse Project validated the potential of towing a delta-wing vehicle to altitude for use as a launch platform. NICHOLAS A. VERONICO

F-4D 65-0714 made its first flight on September 17, 1966. The Phantom flew with the 171st Fighter Interceptor Squadron until the type was phased out in 1990 in favor of newer F-16 Fighting Falcons. F-4D 65-0714 arrived at AMARG on January 19, 1990, and looks remarkably well for having sat in the sun for nearly twenty-four years. To the left is F-4E 67-0223, which last flew with the 35th Tactical Fighter Wing, and to the rear is F-4E 66-0330 from the 35th Tactical Training Wing. Both units flew from George AFB in California. NICHOLAS A. VERONICO

F-4 Phantom tails as far as the eye can see. From left: F-4D 65-0738 last flew with the 136th Fighter Interceptor Squadron of the New York ANG, wears Niagara Falls titles above the fin flash, and arrived at AMARG on June 13, 1990; F-4D 66-7478 is a 178th Fighter Interceptor Squadron Phantom from the Happy Hooligans of North Dakota, which arrived for storage on March 12, 1990; tail code PN is F-4E 72-0165 from the 3rd Tactical Fighter Wing, Clark AFB, Philippines, which arrived at AMARG on March 25, 1991; two unidentified F-4s; and F-4D 66-7464, which made its first flight on January 2, 1967 (this version of the F-4 last served with the 171st Fighter Squadron, 191st Fighter Group, Michigan Air National Guard). NICHOLAS A. VERONICO

One of the most photographed Phantoms in AMARG has to be F-4S BuNo 155539, which last operated with Air Test and Evaluation Squadron Four (VX-4), based at Naval Air Station Point Mugu, California. This aircraft was originally built as an F-4J and made its first flight on February 22, 1968. It was upgraded to F-4S configuration at NAS North Island, California, in May 1981. The Playboy F-4 came to AMARG on May 2, 1986, and VX-4 was disestablished in 1994. NICHOLAS A. VERONICO

When it was first parked in the desert on October 9, 1992, this combat-veteran Phantom was one of the most colorful USAF jets in the boneyard. In August 1990, RF-4C 65-0843 deployed with its unit, the 106th TRS of the Alabama ANG, to Sheikh Isa Air Base, Bahrain, in support of Operation Desert Shield. Throughout Operation Desert Storm and the remainder of the First Gulf War, this Phantom flew tactical reconnaissance missions, including searching for elusive mobile Scud missile launchers. Back home in Birmingham, it became the aircraft that displayed markings to honor the seventy-fifth anniversary of the unit, which had been organized at Kelly Field, Texas, as the 106th Aero Squadron in August 1917. Unfortunately, time and the desert sun have completely faded much of the artwork, including the colorful legend "1917 Diamond Jubilee 1992" across the spine of the jet. Also now gone is the "Recce Rebels" nose art. Faded away large art on the left intake is "1917 Jennies To Jets 1992 Birmingham 106 RS," while on the tail the legend "Diamond Jubilee" is nearly gone. Also under the spraylat on the nose is a fearsome shark mouth. JIM DUNN

MP TYPE 4000
09 NOV 1999

MP TYPE 2000
MAY 29 97

MP TYPE 2000
8 DEC.97

This lineup of German Luftwaffe F-4F Phantoms arrived at AMARG in early January 2005 in the markings of the USAF 20th Fighter Squadron, the unit that they served in at Holloman AFB, New Mexico. The 20th was the host unit for the German Air Force Tactical Training Center established at Holloman AFB on May 1, 1996, to train German crews in the Phantom. Known as the Silver Lobos, these aircraft also carry names in the yellow band above the rudder. This lineup includes F-4F 72-1221 *Pollito*, originally delivered as Luftwaffe 38+11; 72-1200 *Pony Express*, delivered as 37+90; and the squadron's flagship, 72-1163 *Chappie*, delivered as 37+53. Note the different applications of the aircraft's unit and serial number on the tail. JIM DUNN / NICHOLAS A. VERONICO

When the 117th Tactical Reconnaissance Wing of the Alabama Air National Guard retired the RF-4C in 1994, the unit commemorated the occasion with this special "Phantom Pharewell" paint scheme proclaiming "Phantoms Pho Ever." RF-4C 64-1057 was the first reconnaissance Phantom received by the unit and the last one to be retired. RF-4C 64-1057 arrived at the boneyard on May 26, 1994. NICHOLAS A. VERONICO

Air Force RF-4C 69-0359 flew its maiden flight on March 13, 1970, and its last operational outfit before retirement on August 27, 1991, was the 91st Tactical Reconnaissance Squadron of the 67th Tactical Reconnaissance Wing at Bergstrom AFB, Texas. It is seen on the AMARG ramp in March 2010, having returned from a drone deployment.
NICHOLAS A. VERONICO

Hundreds of Air Force pilots learned to fly supersonic in AT-38B 64-13276. This Talon last served with the 433rd Tactical Fighter Training Squadron, 479th Tactical Training Wing, tail code HM. The aircraft was retired to AMARG on August 23, 1991. Notice the AMARG inventory number, TF-108, on the fuselage between the wing and the horizontal stabilizer. NICHOLAS A. VERONICO

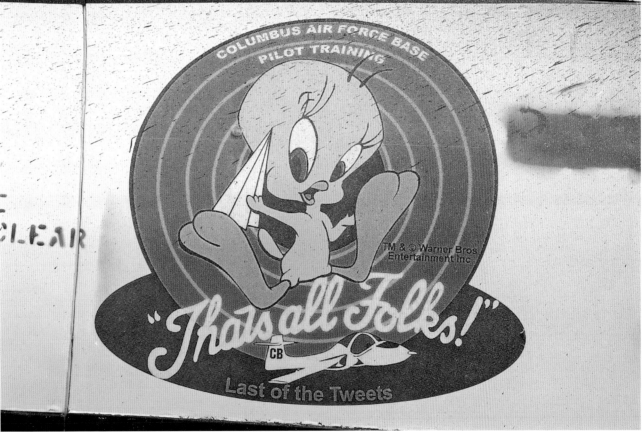

Cessna T-37B 68-8068 was delivered to Columbus AFB, Mississippi, on September 25, 1969, with 9.1 hours of flight time to begin its role to support the Specialized Undergraduate Pilot Training (SUPT) mission. On April 3, 2008, instructor Maj. Robert McGrath and student Capt. Jay Labrum flew the final SUPT mission at Columbus AFB with the *That's All Folks* nose art applied on 68-8068 for this occasion. The aircraft completed 10,351 SUPT sorties and had 16,637.6 hours on its airframe. Since the T-37 is called the Tweet, it is only natural that Tweety Bird would be its mascot, and Warner Bros. Entertainment has often permitted units to make use of the image. Seen here in March 2010, T-37B 68-8068 is crated and set to begin a journey to South America to start a new career with another air force. JIM DUNN

Carrying the name *City of Clovis* on its nose gear doors, F-111F 74-0178 last flew with the 27th Fighter Wing based at Cannon AFB outside Clovis, New Mexico. Prior to this, the aircraft served with the 494th Tactical Fighter Squadron of the 48th Tactical Fighter Wing at RAF Lakenheath in the United Kingdom. While with this squadron, it was deployed to Taif in southwestern Saudi Arabia for bombing missions during Operation Desert Storm, attacking airfields, bridges, bunkers, tanks, and command facilities. This F-111F completed fifty-six combat missions—the most for any aircraft in the 48th. The aircraft was retired on July 29, 1996, with just over 5,200 hours of flight time. JIM DUNN

F-105D 59-1771 *Dynamic Duo II* featured the Rocky and Bullwinkle cartoon characters. This Thunderchief last served with the 149th Tactical Fighter Squadron (Virginia ANG), where T/Sgt. Bernard "Beetle" Bailey applied the artwork. F-105D 59-1771 is now on display at the Air Force Armament Museum at Eglin AFB, Florida.
ARMAND H. VERONICO

Golden Gun was worn by F-105D 61-0164 (149th Tactical Fighter Squadron, Virginia ANG), which arrived for storage on June 17, 1981. On January 16, 1998, the Thunderchief was transferred to Western International Aviation, which prepared the aircraft for display and transport to Hunter Memorial Park in Douglasville, Georgia. This nose art was also painted by Beetle Bailey, who painted the majority of the Virginia ANG's F-105s and A-7s.
ARMAND H. VERONICO

Another Beetle Bailey nose art painting: *Ye Old War Horse* (F-105D 60-0492). This aircraft was transferred to the Valiant Air Command Museum in Titusville, Florida, for display on July 31, 2002.
KAREN B. HAACK

Superhog adorned the side of F-105D 59-1822, which also served with the 149th Tactical Fighter Squadron, Virginia ANG. *Superhog* was one of more than thirty Thunderchiefs painted by Beetle Bailey. On May 24, 1999, this aircraft was transferred from AMARG to the Imperial War Museum at Duxford, England. During Vietnam, this Thunderchief was flown by Maj. (later Gen.) Donald J. Kutyna with the 44th Tactical Fighter Squadron at Takhli Royal Thai Air Force Base in Thailand with the name *The Polish Glider*, a play on Kutyna's heritage as well as the engine-out performance of the aircraft. Kutyna flew 120 combat missions during the war. In 2010, the Thunderjet was moved to the Polish Aviation Museum (Muzeum Lotnictwa Polskiego) in Cracow. KAREN B. HAACK

F-111E 68-0029 came to AMARG on November 18, 1993, having last served with the 55th Fighter Squadron, 20th Fighter Wing, stationed at Upper Heyford, England. During Desert Storm, this aircraft and twenty-seven others from the 55th, 77th, and 79th Fighter Squadrons deployed from Upper Heyford to fly missions from Incirlik Air Base in Turkey. NICHOLAS A. VERONICO

Tail markings on Jacksonville-based F-15C 78-0491 display the colors of the 159th Fighter Squadron, 125th Fighter Wing, Florida ANG. This Eagle arrived at AMARG on September 8, 2010. Before protecting the skies over Florida, 78-0491 flew with the 67th Fighter Squadron, 18th Wing, at Kadena Air Base, Okinawa, Japan. NICHOLAS A. VERONICO

Air Combat Command F-15C Eagle 79-0080 last flew with the 58th Fighter Squadron, 33rd Fighter Wing, at Eglin AFB, Florida. This Desert Storm veteran arrived at AMARG on July 22, 2009. The 58th Fighter Squadron phased the F-15 out in the fall of 2009 and became the first F-35 Lightning II training squadron in October of that year. Note the spray-painted preservation information on the left. Type 1000 denotes that the fighter will be kept in long-term storage, intact, with the potential that the plane may be recalled to service. NICHOLAS A. VERONICO

F-16 Fighting Falcons as far as the eye can see, August 2012. From right to left: F-16 from the 122nd Fighter Wing, Indiana ANG, "Black Snakes" (which exchanged its Fighting Falcons for the A-10 Thunderbolt II in 2010); 83-0162 of the 148th Fighter Squadron, Minnesota ANG; two unidentified Vermont ANG F-16s; 80-0541 from the 177th Fighter Wing, New Jersey ANG; an unidentified F-16; and a fiscal year 1982 F-16 from the Arizona ANG.

NICHOLAS A. VERONICO

Grumman A-6E Bureau of Aeronautics serial number (Buno) 159579 is the air group commander's aircraft from Carrier Air Wing 14 (CAW-14) that was embarked on the USS *Carl Vinson* (CVN-70). This A-6E was assigned to Medium Attack Squadron 196 (VA-196) and arrived at AMARG on March 4, 1997. In spite of its colorful air group markings on the tail, the fuselage markings are low-visibility. NICHOLAS A. VERONICO

A-6E Intruder tails, from left: A-6E Buno 157004, formerly with VA-95, arrived at AMARG on February 23, 1995; A-6E Buno 154156, a VA-196 veteran (note the NK tail code), arrived on January 16, 1996; another A-6E from VA-196, Buno 151573, which arrived on January 18, 1995; and A-6E Buno 152614 from VA-52, which arrived on January 18, 1995. NICHOLAS A. VERONICO

Grumman F-14D Tomcat 164602 last flew with Fighter Squadron 213 (VF-213), The Black Lions, based ashore at NAS Oceana in Virginia. This D model F-14 was delivered to the Navy on May 1, 1992, and flew with VF-2 until 1999, when it transferred to VF-213. During Operation Iraqi Freedom, VF-213 was a component of Carrier Air Wing Eight (CVW-8) on board the USS *Theodore Roosevelt* (CVN-71), and 164602 served as the squadron commander's aircraft. This may be one of the last Tomcats to leave AMARG as it is parked outside the offices of the Navy representatives. NICHOLAS A. VERONICO

Making its home on AMARG's Celebrity Row is Grumman F-14A Tomcat Buno 161866, wearing the markings of VF-154 Black Knights, which last operated aboard the USS *Kitty Hawk* (CV-63). This Tomcat arrived for storage on October 23, 2004. Behind the Tomcat is the fourth Boeing 727 built, 727-022 N7004U (manufacturers' serial number 18296), held in storage for the Smithsonian. The tri-jet arrived at AMARG on November 9, 1994.

NICHOLAS A. VERONICO

F/A-18A Buno 162468 arrived for storage on September 1, 2004. The Hornet wears the colors of Marine Fighter Attack Squadron 321 (VMFA-321). Known as Hell's Angels, the squadron was established on February 1, 1943, at MCAS Cherry Point, North Carolina, flying the Grumman F4F Wildcat and later the Vought F4U Corsair. The unit later flew the F8F Bearcat, A-1 Skyraider, FJ-4 Fury, and F-4 Phantom. VMFA-321 began flying the Hornet in 1991 and made a number of deployments to Europe, before being disestablished on September 11, 2004.

NICHOLAS A. VERONICO

F/A-18A Buno 162879 wears the colors of Naval Strike and Air Warfare Center (NSAWC), based at NAS Fallon, Nevada. This aggressor-marked F/A-18A previously served with the "World Famous Golden Dragons" of VFA-192 at NAF Atsugi, Japan. It was retired on November 4, 2004. NICHOLAS A. VERONICO

F/A-18B Buno 161711 currently lives on AMARG's Celebrity Row and can be seen from the bus tour hosted by the Pima Air & Space Museum. The two-seat Hornet's last assignment was with the U.S. Navy Flight Demonstration Squadron, The Blue Angels. The number-seven jet is used for media orientation flights and can be inserted into the airshow act should an aircraft have a mechanical issue that can't be repaired before show time. Buno 161711 was retired on June 29, 2010. NICHOLAS A. VERONICO

The Salty Dogs of Air Test and Evaluation Squadron 23 (VX-23) are based at NAS Patuxent River, Maryland. The squadron is responsible for determining aircraft-handling qualities for both new models, most recently the X-32, and X-35/F-35 Joint Strike Fighter prototypes. In addition, all modifications made to fixed-wing aircraft are flown and evaluated by the squadron. NFA-18A Buno 162445 was flown by VX-23 until its retirement on March 24, 2005. NICHOLAS A. VERONICO

Bagged B-1B 85-0086 arrived at AMARG on September 11, 2002, and was placed into long-term storage. These aircraft can easily be recalled to service, and if that call never comes, they can be moved to the parts-reclamation area with others of their type. Unfortunately for 85-0086, that call never came, and the aircraft was moved into the boneyard, where it began giving up parts to keep others flying. This aircraft wears the Steve Barba–painted nose art of *Intimidator*, a bobcat thrusting its right paw toward the viewer. In the background is B-1B 86-0096 *Wolf Pack*. (See next page for more photos.) NICHOLAS A. VERONICO

37

All of the Lancers with the 96th Bomb Wing at Dyess AFB were reassigned to the 7th Bomb Wing on October 1, 1993, when that unit relocated from Carswell AFB, Texas, and the 96th Bomb Wing was inactivated. At the time B-1B 84-0058 was known as the *Master of Disaster* when it became a new member of the 9th Bomb Squadron. The Bats of the 9th BS flew B-1B 84-0058 until it was retired on August 26, 2002, wearing the name *Eternal Guardian*.
RON STRONG

The first Rockwell B-1B Lancer was delivered to the U.S. Air Force in June 1985. The type was brought into service to modernize the Air Force's strategic nuclear bomber fleet with an aircraft that was capable of Mach 1+ speeds and able to penetrate Soviet radar defenses, deliver bombs on target, and return. The end of the Cold War saw the B-1B begin flying its first conventional bombing missions in support of Operation Desert Fox in December 1998. B-1B 84-0055 *Lethal Weapon* last served with the 28th Bomb Squadron, 7th Bomb Wing, at Dyess AFB, Texas, and was delivered to storage on September 3, 2002.
JIM DUNN

The principal reason for the return of nose art on U.S. Air Force aircraft in the mid-1980s was to pay respect to the aircraft and crews of World War II. Before the use of the female form became frowned upon, B-1B 84-0050 proudly carried the nose art *Surprise Attack*, which had flown on B-24M 44-50956 in the China-Burma-India theater during World War II. Retired on November 1, 2002, 84-0050 displays the more politically correct *DAWG B-ONE* nose art. JIM DUNN

In 1996, B-1B 85-0092 was reassigned from the 28th Bomb Wing at Ellsworth AFB, South Dakota, to join the 128th Bomb Squadron of the Georgia ANG at its new home of Robins AFB. Formerly the 128th Fighter Squadron operating the F-15A Eagle, this Georgia unit would become the second squadron in the ANG to be assigned the B-1B Lancer. (The other squadron was the 127th Bomb Squadron of the Kansas ANG.) On September 17, 2002, *Apocalypse*—which had previously carried the names *Enforcer* and *The Uninvited*—departed Robins AFB on its retirement flight as the final B-1B Lancer to serve in the ANG. JIM DUNN

During a training flight on the night of October 14, 1990, B-1B 86-0128, then assigned to the 28th Bomb Squadron of the 384th Bomb Wing at McConnell AFB, Kansas, suffered a catastrophic failure of an engine blade in the number-one engine. The blades severed the engine mounts, causing the engine to depart from the aircraft and forcing the crew to make an emergency landing in Pueblo, Colorado. After extensive repairs that included the removal of the wings and nacelles, the aircraft returned to service. It was later assigned to the 37th Bomb Squadron of the 28th Bomb Wing at Ellsworth AFB, South Dakota, and was subsequently retired on March 31, 2003. Prior to being given the *Fury 1* nose art, it carried the names *The Hawk, Miss Behavin', Boss, Pony Soldier, Striking Distance,* and *Dakota Fury.* JIM DUNN

OP TYPE 4000
31 JULY 03

Countless aircraft have worn the nose art *Lucky 13*, from B-17s and B-29s to B-52s and B-1B 84-0053. This Lancer last flew with the 28th Bomb Squadron, 7th Bomb Wing, Dyess AFB, Texas, and was retired on January 6, 2003. Today it sits in the parts-reclamation area providing components to keep other Lancers in the air. Note the AMARG inventory number, AABT0013, under the cockpit window (below). JIM DUNN AND RON STRONG

Sitting in the parts-reclamation area is B-1B 84-0056, which arrived on August 20, 2002, from the 28th Bomb Squadron, 7th Bomb Wing, Dyess AFB (note the DY tail code). This aircraft has given up its radome, nose landing gear, and horizontal stabilizers. Additional parts sit in the white boxes near the wooden braces that keep the aircraft level. This Lancer was known as *Sweet Sixteen*. The comparison photos show how quick nose art fades in the harsh Arizona sun.
NICHOLAS A. VERONICO

Two rows of B-1Bs: one set has the potential to return to flight while the other eight Lancers' flying days are over. Note the different tail flashes and codes for bombers from Dyess, Ellsworth, and Georgia. NICHOLAS A. VERONICO

The first B-1B arrived at Dyess AFB to join the 96th Bomb Wing on June 29, 1985. The 96th would receive twenty-eight of the first twenty-nine production Lancers and become the first B-1B wing to gain initial operating capability on October 1, 1986. The fourteenth Lancer off the production line was B-1B 84-0054, which joined the 337th Bomb Squadron of the 96th. During its career at Dyess, it wore the names *Tasmanian Terror, Silver Bullet,* and finally *Rage* when it was retired from the 28th Bomb Squadron on September 18, 2002. JIM DUNN

Right and left sides of the forward fuselage of B-1B 85-0071 *Mr. Bones* from the 116th Bomb Wing of the Georgia ANG, stationed at Robbins AFB. *Mr. Bones* arrived at AMARG on August 23, 2002, and made the wing's last flight before it transitioned into a new role as the 116th Air Control Wing, flying the E-8C Joint Surveillance Target Attack Radar System (JSTARS) aircraft. NICHOLAS A. VERONICO

Rockwell B-1B Lancer 85-0067 wears *On Defense* nose art of a bald eagle in front of a waving American flag and the 28th Bomb Squadron, 7th Bomb Wing's insignia. This aircraft was last operated by the 419th Flight Test Squadron, 412th Test Wing, at Edwards AFB, California, which did not change its markings. The Lancer arrived for storage on March 25, 2003. NICHOLAS A. VERONICO

Ellsworth-based B-1B 85-0060 flies with the 34th Bomb Sqaudron, 28th Bomb Wing, and is seen on the ramp at AMARG in March 2010. The squadron began flying the B-1B in 1994. Lancers from the 34th Bomb Squadron opened Operation Iraqi Freedom when four of its aircraft dropped nearly 100 2,000-pound GBU-31 JDAM (Joint Direct Air Munition) bombs. NICHOLAS A. VERONICO

Artist Steve Barba painted B-1B 86-0096 *Wolf Pack*. This Lancer was retired on September 17, 2002, having served with the 37th Bomb Squadron, 28th Bomb Wing, at Ellsworth AFB, South Dakota. NICHOLAS A. VERONICO

Insignia of the 77th Bomb Squadron is shown on the left forward fuselage of B-1B 86-0097. The bomber flew from Ellsworth AFB to AMARG for storage on April 30, 2003. NICHOLAS A. VERONICO

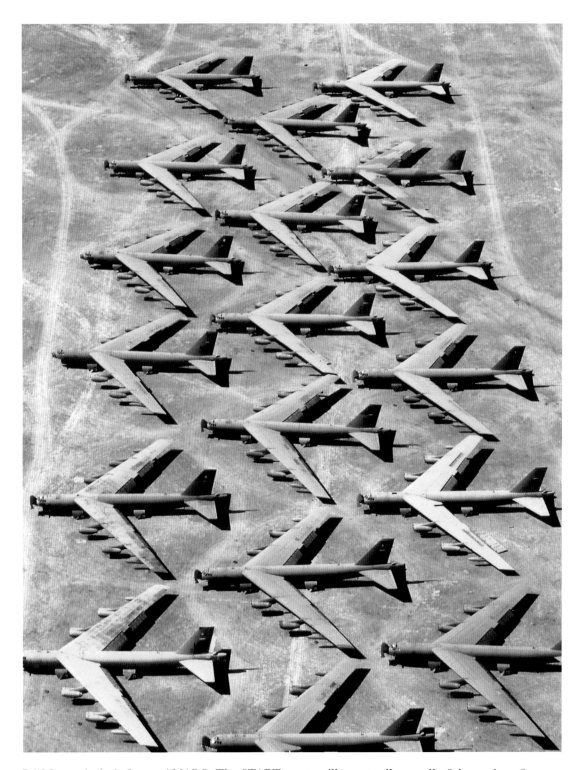

B-52Gs await their fate at AMARG. The START treaty will eventually see all of these aircraft surgically cut into five sections—nose, center section, right and left wings, and tail—and pushed together to enable Russian satellites to verify their destruction. Once the bombers have been picked clean, they are shredded and recycled. NICHOLAS A. VERONICO

B-52G 58-0249 last flew during a time when nose art was frowned upon. The bomber was named *Urban Renewal*, but the name was carried only on the left side of the fuselage in the space reserved for the crew names. This B-52G arrived at AMARG on September 10, 1991, and last flew with the 379th Bomb Wing at Wurtsmith AFB, Michigan. During World War II, planes from the 379th were identified by the Triangle K on the tail, and its appearance on the Stratofortress is a nod of recognition to those crews who flew the B-17 in combat. NICHOLAS A. VERONICO

B-52G 59-2566 was known as *The Wild Potato* when it flew missions in Desert Storm. Its last assignment was with the 2nd Bomb Wing at Barksdale AFB, Louisiana. It arrived for storage on September 16, 1992, and was sectioned to comply with the START treaty on May 29, 2001. The pilots' seats have been removed and are sitting on a pallet in front of the nose section. NICHOLAS A. VERONICO

Last flown by the 93rd Bomb Wing at Castle AFB, California, B-52G 59-2599 has donated its engines and avionics to the flying B-52 fleet. Notice the line of bomb symbols denoting this aircraft's participation in Desert Storm. Its missions were from the island of Diego Garcia as part of the 4300th Bomb Wing (Provisional). The bomber arrived at AMARG on March 15, 1994 with 15,531.6 hours total time. NICHOLAS A. VERONICO

In 2013, B-52G 58-0206 took up residence on AMARG's Celebrity Row and can be seen on the AMARG bus tour operated by the Pima Air & Space Museum. While bombing targets during Desert Storm, this Stratofortress wore the names *Cultured Vulture* and *Texas Ranger.* Its last assignment was with the aircrew training squadron, part of the 93rd Bomb Wing at Castle AFB, California. The aircraft arrived for storage on February 1, 1994 with 14,355 hours total time. NICHOLAS A. VERONICO

When the 43rd Bombardment Wing based at Andersen AFB on Guam converted from the nuclear to the conventional bombing mission in 1988, it received several B-52G aircraft already configured for the conventional role. One of those aircraft coming to Guam was B-52G 58-0224, which had been serving with the 42nd Bombardment Wing at Loring AFB, Maine. On the tail of the aircraft the palm tree symbol of the 60th Bomb Squadron now replaced the outline of the state of Maine that was carried by Loring AFB B-52Gs. All of this was short-lived, however, as the 43rd inactivated in 1990, and B-52G 58-0224 was placed into storage on February 12, 1990, with a total of 13,078.8 hours of service. JIM DUNN

The first B-52H arrived at AMARG on July 24, 2008. Since that time, two dozen more have followed the initial aircraft into storage. Note the mix of aircraft from Barksdale, Louisiana (tail code LA), and Minot, North Dakota (MT), as well as the differing styles in the application of the aircraft's serial number and the tail flashes.
NICHOLAS A. VERONICO

B-52H 61-0023 was the first H model retired to AMARG. These aircraft are being kept in flyable storage while the remaining B-52 yield parts for the Stratofortress fleet. After it was delivered to the Air Force, B-52H 61-0023 was bailed back to Boeing for testing under an Air Force Systems Command contract to gather structural load data.

On January 10, 1964, the crew, led by Charles Fisher, was flying at low levels to simulate a bomber penetrating Soviet airspace flying under its radar screen, approximately 1,000 feet above the ground at 345 knots, when the aircraft flew into turbulence which quickly yawed the aircraft to the left, then to the right, coupled with a roll to the right. The crew called for assistance and a Boeing-operated F-100 arrived and informed the crew that 83 percent of the tail had been torn off. The flight test crew

of four Boeing employees were able to control the aircraft by vectoring engine thrust and using the air brakes. After more than five hours in the air with its tail missing, the crew landed the aircraft without incident at Blytheville AFB, Arkansas. The aircraft was repaired, and all other B-52s had their tail structures strengthened. Eventually, 61-0023 was repaired and returned to the Air Force's fleet and served without further incident for more than forty years.

Note that the aircraft was originally photographed covered in spraylat (March 2010) and again in August 2012, with its wing and sword nose art *Dimico Delectus* ("I choose to lead the fight") exposed during represervation. NICHOLAS A. VERONICO / HISTORIC PHOTOS COURTESY OF U.S. AIR FORCE & BOEING

B-52Hs with a variety of cruise-missile and iron-bomb mission markings. B-52H 61-0027 made its first flight on May 11, 1962, and was flown to AMARG on January 21, 2009. During its career, it wore the names *The Bull* and *Land Scaper II*. The second aircraft in the row, 61-0024, made its first flight on April 20, 1962, and its final name was *Hell Razor*. This aircraft arrived for storage on January 6, 2009. NICHOLAS A. VERONICO

Unfortunately for historians, many warplanes in the post–World War II era have not always retained their mission markings throughout their service career. Often when an aircraft is transferred or repainted, these markings are removed or never reapplied. For B-52H 60-0020, the flagship of the 20th Bomb Squadron based with the 2nd Bomb Wing at Barksdale AFB, Louisiana, the eight bombing missions remaining on it when it was retired on September 4, 2008, do not represent the total combat record of this aircraft. Named *The Mad Bolshevik*, 60-0020 was deployed to RAF Fairford in the United Kingdom from February 21 to June 23, 1999, to support Operation Noble Anvil—part of the NATO Operation Allied Force in Kosovo—during which it conducted twenty bombing missions, including the launch of ten conventional air-launched cruise missiles (CALCM). This mission tally was the second highest of any B-52 in the operation. JIM DUNN

B-52H 61-0034 also served the U.S. Air Force. This Stratofortress made its first flight on July 5, 1962, and was delivered to the Air Force on August 13 of that year. On August 14, 2008, forty-six years later, it flew to storage. During its long career, the aircraft was known as *Predator*, *Checkmate*, and finally *Wise Guy*. NICHOLAS A. VERONICO

B-52H 61-0027 wears eight iron-bomb and eight cruise-missile mission marks denoting its service with the "Bomber Barons" of the 23rd Bomb Squadron, 5th Bomb Wing, during air campaigns in the new millennium. The 23rd continues to fly the B-52H from Minot AFB. This aircraft was retired on January 21, 2009.
JIM DUNN AND NICHOLAS A. VERONICO

June 19, 1961, saw B-52H 60-0030 lift off from the Wichita, Kansas, runway for the first time. Known as *Luck O'
The Irish*, the Stratofortress last flew out of Barksdale AFB, Louisiana, and was retired on August 21, 2008.
NICHOLAS A. VERONICO

A late-afternoon thunderstorm produces a bolt of lightning that touched down behind rows of ex–U.S. Navy P-3 Orion antisubmarine patrol aircraft. To the right is long-time AMARG resident P-3A Buno 151378, last stationed at Naval Air Rework Facility Jacksonville, Florida. This Orion arrived at AMARG on September 2, 1986, and is seen in August 2012. NICHOLAS A. VERONICO

A row of eleven of the more than 150 P-3s in storage at AMARG, as seen in August 2012. Closest to the camera is P-3B Buno 153420, which last served with Patrol Squadron 90 (VP-90), a reserve squadron stationed at NAS Glenview, Illinois. Buno 153420 was flown to storage on January 13, 1994, and the squadron was disestablished on September 30, 1994. NICHOLAS A. VERONICO

Retired on December 6, 1985, P-3A Buno 151383 wears the tail code PG and faded fuselage markings from VP-65 ("The Tridents") from NAS Point Mugu, California. VP-65 was disestablished March 31, 2006. In the past, Buno 151383 had served with VP-64 ("The Condors") from NAS Willow Grove, Pennsylvania, and wore the large tail markings of that squadron for a number of years. NICHOLAS A. VERONICO

RP-3A Buno 149670 wears the markings of the Naval Research Laboratory along with a large radar canoe extending from the forward bomb bay. Previously, this aircraft also flew with a large, possibly side-looking radar antenna on top of the fuselage. In the mid- to late-1980s, Buno 149670 was involved in a number of weather-related experiments known as FASINEX (Frontal Air-Sea Interaction Experiment). This Orion arrived at AMARG on May 19, 1994. NICHOLAS A. VERONICO

NP-3D Buno 148889 was delivered to the U.S. Navy on April 15, 1962, and served almost exclusively as a test aircraft from day one. Buno 148889 was the S-3A avionics test bed, served at the NAWC-AD detachment at NAS Willow Grove as the Over The Horizon–Targeting (OTHT) test-and-development aircraft, was assigned to the Naval Force Aircraft Test Squadron (NFATS), and in 2002 joined the Naval Test Pilot School at NAS Patuxent River's aircraft fleet. After forty-six years, Buno 148889 was sent to AMARG on October 22, 2008, and was stricken from the Navy's inventory on May 6, 2009. NICHOLAS A. VERONICO

RP-3D Buno 152738 wears shark eyes and mouth on its nose. This Orion was delivered to the Navy's VP-9 on May 6, 1966. A decade later, in September 1976, she was transferred to VP-8 and flew as *City of Augusta*. She then flew with VP-62 and VP-94 before being modified into UP-3B configuration. In July 1991, Buno 152738 joined Navy Oceanographic Development Squadron Eight (VXN-8) and was subsequently reconfigured as an RP-3D for Project Birdseye and Seascan. The aircraft was flown to AMARG for storage on December 1, 1993. RON STRONG

From 1984 to 2004, Lockheed UP-3A Orion Buno 150495 served at NAS Keflavik, Iceland, flying as the commander's aircraft. The patrol plane served as the base hack, wearing the name *Valkyrja*. On January 28, 2004, she arrived at AMARG for storage. RON STRONG

Lockheed UP-3A Orion Buno 150528 was delivered to the U.S. Navy on December 19, 1963. In order, the Orion served with VP-19, VP-6, VP-28, VP-4, VP-31, VP-4 again, VQ-1, and finally with VXN-8, where she gained the name and artwork of *Loon*. The plane was stored on April 18, 1990. RON STRONG

Lockheed antisubmarine and maritime patrol P-3C (Update III) Buno 158566 last operated with VP-16 and was retired to AMARG on February 18, 2004. The aircraft is seen under overhaul to return it to service. From AMARG, it was flown to Lockheed Martin's Greenville, South Carolina–facility for modernization before it joined 133 Squadron of the Republic of China Navy in Taiwan. NICHOLAS A. VERONICO

Former Canadian Navy CP-140A Arcturus serial number 140121 was acquired directly from Lockheed on October 19, 1990. Its U.S. civil registration, most likely a ferry permit, was N65672. The aircraft joined 14 Wing at Canadian Forces Base Greenwood, Nova Scotia, Canada, where it flew long-range patrols over the Atlantic. CP-140A 140121 was withdrawn from use and stored at AMARG in January 2011. NICHOLAS A. VERONICO

Lockheed SP-2H Buno 148340 last served with VP-94 and arrived at AMARG on July 22, 1976. The mid-1950s vintage patrol bomber is held in storage for the National Museum of Naval Aviation, Pensacola, Florida.
NICHOLAS A. VERONICO

Seen in its final glory as the CAG bird of Sea Control Squadron VS-31, S-3B Viking 159732 takes pride of place on AMARG's Celebrity Row. "The Topcats" of VS-31 last served with Carrier Air Wing Nine (CVW-9) aboard the USS *John C. Stennis* and were shore-based at NAS Jacksonville, from which 159732 was flown into retirement on April 1, 2008, when the unit was inactivated. The Viking was nicknamed the "Hoover" because of the vacuum cleaner–like sounds produced by its engines; less than a handful continue in Navy service as missile range control aircraft.
JIM DUNN

The unique tail markings of VRC-50, tail code RG, decorate Lockheed US-3A Buno 157994. This aircraft was flown to AMARG on August 10, 1995, and looks in fairly good condition with only its engines and nose radome missing in this March 2010 photo. NICHOLAS A. VERONICO

Lockheed's S-3 Viking has been used in a number of roles; however, it was built as a carrier-based antisubmarine platform. The Maulers of Sea Control Squadron Three Two (VS-32) flew S-3B Buno 160134 from the decks of the USS *Enterprise* (CVN-65). When shore-based, VS-32 flew from NAS Jacksonville. The squadron was disestablished on September 25, 2008, and Buno 160134 arrived for storage five days later on September 30. NICHOLAS A. VERONICO

CHAPTER 3

TANKER AND TRANSPORT ART

In September 2009, when the final KC-135Es in service were departing their squadrons for the last time, it would not be the end of their contribution to the USAF. Several were flown to Shepard AFB in Wichita Falls, Texas, to serve as maintenance trainers, while those that went to AMARG will be supplying parts to keep the remainder of the KC-135 fleet flying for another twenty years or more. Making its final flight to AMARG from the 108th Air Refueling Squadron (ARS) at Scott AFB, Illinois, on February 12, 2008, KC-135E 58-0024 *American Made* features nose art by Marc Sova that provides an image very representative of the service of the KC-135.

NICHOLAS A. VERONICO / RON STRONG

In its service career from July 1982 until September 2009, during which they only served in Air Force Reserve and Air National Guard squadrons, the KC-135E became the canvas for some of the largest and most elaborate nose art creations in the modern era. Some of the more elaborate examples have been painted by Donna Pitaro on the KC-135Es of the 171st Air Refueling Wing of the Pennsylvania ANG. Using a variety of local and patriotic themes, she often covered all of the available area on the nose of the tanker for her creations. Representing one of her local subjects, KC-135E 57-1423 *Allegheny Warrior* was assigned to the 147th ARS when it departed its Pittsburgh base for the final time on June 6, 2007. JIM DUNN

During the period that the KC-135E served in the Air National Guard, the vast majority of its air refueling wings had only one flying squadron designated as an air refueling squadron. One of the rare exceptions to this was the 171st Air Refueling Wing of the Pennsylvania ANG, which had the 146th and 147th Air Refueling Squadrons under its control. Both operated out of Greater Pittsburgh International Airport, with KC-135E 56-3626 *America's Heartbeat* assigned to the 146th. It was the good fortune of both of these squadrons to have Donna Pitaro as an artist. *America's Heartbeat* was flown to its new home at Davis-Monthan AFB on August 12, 2009. JIM DUNN

Boeing KC-135E 57-1494 *Fallen Heroes* was originally delivered to the U.S. Air Force on November 19, 1958. The tanker last served with the 126th Air Refueling Wing at Scott AFB, Illinois, where Marc Sova applied this nose art, which includes the insignia of all branches of the U.S. military: Army, Air Force, Coast Guard, Marines, and Navy. KC-135E 57-1494 was retired just short of its fiftieth anniversary on May 13, 2008. RON STRONG

Known as *Balls 3*, KC-135E 58-0003 *Easyrider* was one of the longest-serving E models assigned to the 108th Air Refueling Squadron of the 126th Air Refueling Wing of the Illinois ANG. Today the 108th operates the KC-135R, fitted with the much more powerful CFM International F108-CF-100 turbofan engines. The ANG is now the primary operator of the KC-135R fleet, and along with a few active duty and Air Force Reserve Command (AFRC) units, it will be their responsibility to keep these aged warriors in action. Painted by Marc Sova, *Easyrider* made its last ride on July 11, 2007. JIM DUNN

KC-135E 56-3648 is from the 171st Air Refueling Wing of the Pennsylvania ANG and arrived for storage on May 7, 2004. The Stratotanker wears the name and nose art of *Bad Company*, which features the Tasmanian Devil at work. To use this character, the 171st had to obtain permission from Warner Bros. and add a copyright notification, seen at the right of the art. *Bad Company* was painted by Donna Pitaro.

NICHOLAS A. VERONICO

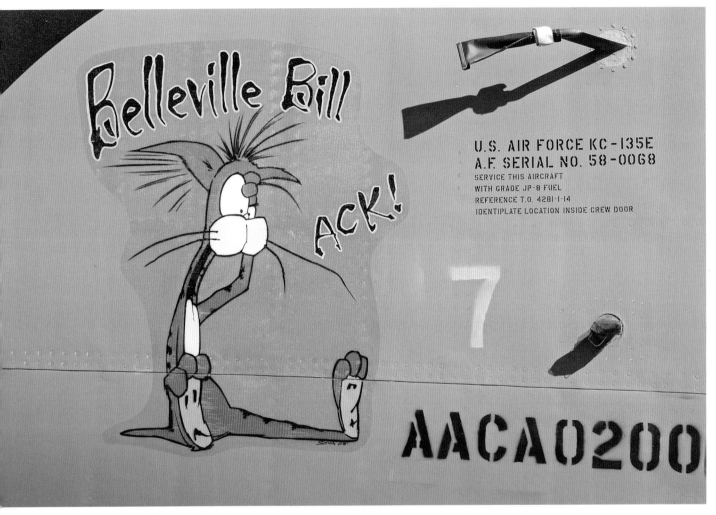

Though KC-135A 58-0068 was serving with the 133rd Air Refueling Squadron of the New Hampshire ANG at Pease AFB prior to modification to become an E model, it was not returned to that unit upon completion of the work. Instead, KC-135E 58-0068 became one of the first of its type to join the 108th Air Refueling Squadron of the Illinois ANG at busy O'Hare International Airport in Chicago. In 1999, the unit relocated to Scott AFB outside Belleville, Illinois, where 58-0068 gained the name *Belleville Bill*, with nose art by Marc Sova. The character, Bill D. Cat, appeared in the cartoonist Berkeley Breathed's *Bloom County* comic strip. The tanker was retired on April 15, 2008. JIM DUNN

The 940th Air Refueling Group (Heavy) was serving at Mather AFB near Sacramento when it was called up for Desert Shield. The unit deployed most of its aircraft and personnel to the 1708th Air Refueling Wing (Provisional) operating out of Jeddah/King Abdul Aziz International Airport in Saudi Arabia. Retired from the 314th Air Refueling Squadron of the 940th Air Refueling Wing at Beale AFB, California, on March 27, 2008, KC-135E 58-0090 *Eagle One* wears appropriate nose art after its many years of service with this Air Force Reserve unit. NICHOLAS A. VERONICO & JIM DUNN

The KC-135 Stratotanker had a long history with the Strategic Air Command (SAC). From its introduction in 1956 until SAC was inactivated on June 1, 1992, the KC-135 shared ramp space with the B-52 Stratofortress on SAC bases throughout the country. KC-135E 59-1479 was assigned to the 146th Aerial Refueling Squadron at Pittsburgh International Airport and wears the nose art of *Falcons Spirit*, painted by Donna Pitaro. This aircraft was flown to storage on April 24, 2007. JIM DUNN

From World War II to the present day, cartoon characters have been some of the most reproduced subjects for nose art, with characters from Walt Disney and Warner Bros. often being the most popular. One of the those famous Warner Bros. characters, Bugs Bunny, leads the way on KC-135E 57-1497 *Fill 'Er Up Doc*. The tanker last served with the 108th Air Refueling Squadron of the Illinois ANG. Based at Scott AFB, *Fill 'Er Up Doc* was sent to AMARG on April 22, 2008. JIM DUNN

Last serving as a KC-135A with the 116th Air Refueling Squadron of the Washington ANG at Fairchild AFB in Spokane, Washington, this Stratotanker was upgraded to KC-135E standards and reassigned to the 151st Air Refueling Squadron of the Tennessee ANG. Here KC-135E 57-1425 gained the name and nose art of *Firebird*. Based at McGhee-Tyson Airport in Knoxville, it served with this unit when it was activated for duty on December 20, 1990, to support Desert Shield. The squadron was released from active duty on April 1, 1992, after Desert Storm brought a conclusion to the First Gulf War. It was retired from the unit on May 20, 2008. JIM DUNN

When an artist is given a nose art project that involves a cartoon character, he may be permitted to use a famous one from Hollywood or the newspapers, or he might call on his own imagination to create one. For the 108th Air Refueling Squadron at Scott AFB in Illinois, artist Marc Sova used Bugs Bunny character on *Fill 'Er Up Doc* and Bill D. Cat on *Belleville Bill*. For KC-135E 57-1480 *Flying Dog*, he came up with another colorful character that hopefully doesn't reflect on the flying characteristics of this aircraft. The *Flying Dog* made it one last time to the boneyard on February 20, 2008. JIM DUNN

It is a tradition in the USAF to "sign off" an aircraft when it is the final one of its type to depart the squadron. Home-based with the 151st Air Refueling Squadron of the Tennessee ANG at McGhee-Tyson ANGB outside of Knoxville, KC-135E 56-3609 *For God and Country* (above) still carries some of the names of those who saw it off on May 30, 2007. This aircraft has an even earlier connection to country music legend Dolly Parton: it carried her name and image prior to receiving the more patriotic *For God and Country*.

JIM DUNN

Before the upswing in patriotic nose art themes, KC-135E 57-1460 carried the cartoon character and name Taz on its nose. Now with the state of Kansas as background and four eagles keeping watch, this tanker took on the title *Four Faces of Freedom* for the remainder of its tour with the 190th Air Refueling Wing of the Kansas ANG. Based at Forbes Field in Topeka and assigned to the 117th Air Refueling Squadron, KC135E 57-1460 went into storage at AMARG on March 19, 2008. JIM DUNN

KC-135E 57-2608 had a long tour with the 171st Air Refueling Wing of the Pennsylvania ANG, during which it picked up the name and Donna Pitaro nose art of *Fuelin' Around*. The tanker was transferred to the 185th Air Refueling Wing of the Iowa ANG, which shortly thereafter began transitioning from the KC-135E to the KC-135R. *Fuelin' Around* was flown to storage on July 23, 2008. NICHOLAS A. VERONICO

Of the 732 KC-135A Stratotankers that Boeing would build in Renton, Washington, for delivery to the USAF, a total of 161 were converted to the KC-135E model. In August 1991, KC-135A 57-2602, while assigned to the active-duty 7th Air Refueling Squadron at Carswell AFB, Texas, would be one of the final A models to be given the E model modifications. At that time, it carried the name *American Maid* and featured nose art of a long-haired redhead wearing a flight suit with an American flag as a background. When reassigned and finally retired by the 150th Air Refueling Squadron of the New Jersey ANG at McGuire AFB on May 4, 2009, it carried the name *Hit That!*, with nose art that was much less memorable than its previous classic pinup style. JIM DUNN

With most of its time since modification as an E model spent with the 147th Air Refueling Squadron in Pittsburgh, KC-135E 59-1457 *Kansas Guardians* was a late arrival to the 117th Air Refueling Squadron in Topeka, Kansas. Spending only a few short years with the squadron, it nevertheless joined other tankers from this unit with nose art honoring those who served the military in Kansas. In particular, it notes the service given by pilots assigned to Strategic Air Command squadrons based at the former Forbes AFB, from which *Kansas Guardians* flew into retirement on June 17, 2008. JIM DUNN

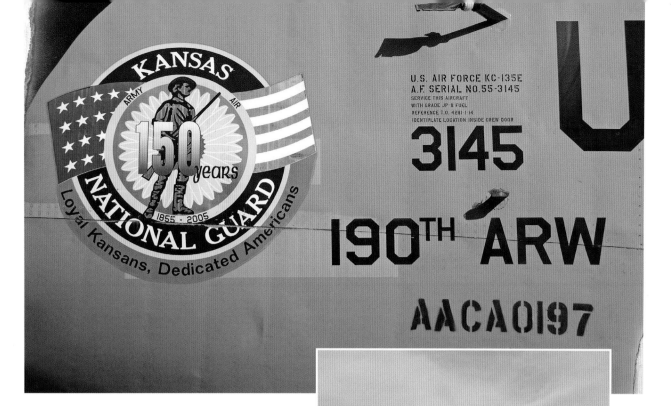

In Fiscal Year 1955, Boeing KC-135A 55-3145 became the next to last in the initial batch of twenty-nine KC-135A Stratotankers ordered by the USAF. After being modified with Pratt & Whitney TF-33 turbofan engines in the 1980s, this aircraft—now KC-135E 55-3145—would serve until its final flight on May 28, 2008. While assigned to the 117th Air Refueling Squadron's "Kansas Coyotes" at Forbes Field in Topeka, KC-135E 55-3145 was given nose art to honor the 150 years of service of the Kansas National Guard and also a special 1956–2006 decal on its tail to commemorate the fiftieth anniversary of the first flight of a Boeing Stratotanker. JIM DUNN

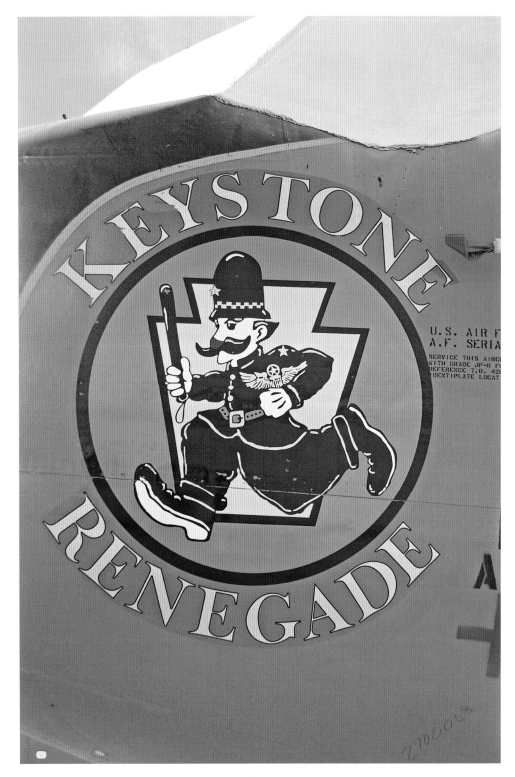

In the past, aircraft unit changes, especially in active-duty squadrons, were a common occurrence. In most cases, an aircraft would not stay with one squadron for long until it was assigned to the Reserve or ANG. For KC-135A 59-1496, the 1980s would see it transferred from the 7th Air Refueling Squadron of the 7th Bomb Wing at Carswell AFB, Texas, to the 924th Air Refueling Squadron of the 93rd Bomb Wing at Castle AFB, California, before becoming a late addition to the KC-135E ANG fleet in the early 1990s. For the final fifteen years of service, it would call the 147th Air Refueling Squadron of the 171st Air Refueling Wing at Pittsburgh its home. Now named *Keystone Renegade*, it departed for Davis-Monthan AFB on May 23, 2007. JIM DUNN

While the hot and dry desert climate of Tucson may provide the best possible outdoor storage site for aircraft, the intensity of direct sunlight on the paint can take a heavy toll. Photographed less than two years after arriving at AMARG for storage on April 24, 2008, KC-135E 60-0327 *Liberties Veil* from the 191st Air Refueling Squadron of the Utah ANG at Salt Lake City shows the damage and fading that will claim it from history in a few short years.
JIM DUNN

After several KC-135A Stratotankers were quickly modified for intelligence gathering, it was decided to use the C-135 airframe for a series of dedicated reconnaissance aircraft. To replace the sixteen RB-50s operated by the Air Photographic and Charting Service, nine RC-135A aircraft were ordered, with a total of four being built and delivered to Turner AFB, Georgia. Operating in the Pacer Swan Program, these aircraft had cameras installed in the forward body fuel tank, but they were built without refueling equipment. Reassigned to the 1370th Photo Mapping Wing at Forbes AFB, Kansas, they would be rendered obsolete by satellites in only a few years. After a stint as staff transports, the four aircraft had refueling equipment added and were redesignated KC-135Ds.

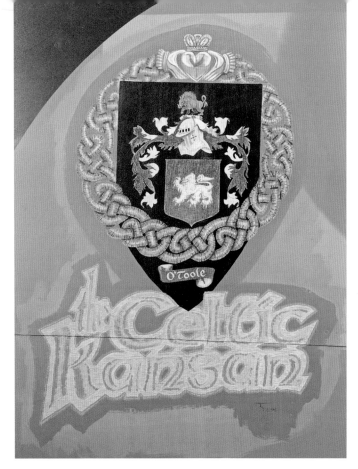

All four, 63-8058 through 63-8061, were included when 157 tankers were re-engined with Pratt & Whitney TF-33 turbofan engines; however, they retained their KC-135D designation (while the others became KC-135Es). Throughout their history, the four aircraft would serve in the same squadrons, with a final reassignment from the 168th Air Refueling Squadron of the Alaska ANG at Eielson AFB, Alaska, to the 117th Air Refueling Squadron of the Kansas ANG at their former home of Forbes Field outside Topeka. KC-135D 63-8058 *Liberty's Guardian* was retired on March 19, 2007, 63-8059 *We Will Not Fail* on March 14, 63-8060 *The Celtic Kansan* on March 28, and *Some Gave All* on April 4. JIM DUNN

In one of the most elaborate and detailed nose art images ever seen, artist Donna Pitaro has incorporated scenes from America's past and present to create a contemporary symbol to honor the meaning of service to the country. While the image on KC-135E 57-1447 *The Patriot* may not be seen by many since it left the 146th Air Refueling Squadron in Pittsburgh on May 9, 2007, its message should continue to be a reminder for all to remember those who serve. JIM DUNN

Another artist with the 171st Air Refueling Wing at Pittsburgh was Larry Hess, who contributed this cartoon caricature to KC-135E 58-0037 *Old Iron*. Though *Old Iron* retired from the 147th Air Refueling Squadron on March 2, 2007, the service history of other KC-135 models may continue for another twenty-five years. Considering that the first production model was delivered to the USAF in June 1957, with the final delivery coming in 1965, the Stratotanker is one of the most significant aircraft ever to serve in the USAF. JIM DUNN / NICHOLAS A. VERONICO

The phrase "Oldie But Goodie" has inspired many different nose art creations over the years. In this case, on KC-135E 57-1464 from the 141st Air Refueling Squadron of the New Jersey ANG at McGuire AFB, it has brought together a trio of classic 1950s Chevrolets at the local filling station. Pride of place in this nose art goes to a two-tone India ivory/pinecrest green 1956 Chevy convertible, with a matador red 1957 and a non-standard yellow 1955 in the background. Being a classic itself from 1957, KC-135E 57-1464 ended its fifty years of service to the USAF and ANG on February 6, 2008. JIM DUNN

Air Force Reserve units have a history of moving from base to base, and KC-135E 61-0268 *Petro Pony* called three bases home during its service as an E model. The 940th Air Refueling Wing might best be known as the nomads of Northern California as they kept moving throughout the area. First established in 1963 as a transport group at McClellan AFB near Sacramento, the unit moved across town to Mather AFB in 1977, gaining the refueling mission at that base. Converting to the KC-135E in 1986, they were forced to leave Mather and return to McClellan in 1993 when Mather closed. When McClellan closed in 1997, the unit moved a few more miles up the road to Beale AFB. Today the 940th Wing operates unmanned RQ-4 Global Hawks after the final tanker departed in May 2008. *Petro Pony* was assigned to their 314th Air Refueling Squadron when it left Beale AFB for the final time on March 18, 2008. JIM DUNN

Incorporated into the nose art on KC-135E 57-1465 *Pit Stop* are the initials NKAWTG, which stand for the unofficial motto of the tanker community: "Nobody Kicks Ass Without Tanker Gas." As of February 2013, the inventory at AMARG showed 106 KC-135E Stratotankers in storage, with 57-1465, which entered the inventory on April 1, 2009, from the 151st Air Refueling Squadron of the Tennessee ANG, not among them. In July 2012, it was removed from the inventory with its disposition currently being undetermined. JIM DUNN

After spending most of its service with the 147th Air Refueling Squadron of the Pennsylvania ANG, KC-135E 59-1484 *POW MIA* made a final brief tour wth the 108th Air Refueling Squadron of the Illinois ANG prior to a July 21, 2009, retirement. While with the 147th Air Refueling Squadron, 59-1484 was a veteran of some difficult Desert Storm combat sorties that may have involved a serious midair collision with an F-111 during a night refueling. The proudly displayed mission markings are mostly lost to history. JIM DUNN

With its tail gone and the windscreens removed as replacements for another Stratotanker, KC-135E 56-3612 *Pittsburgh Panther Pride* is nearing the end of its useful life at AMARG. This tanker and its nose art commemorating athletics at the University of Pittsburgh last flew with the 171st Air Refueling Wing of the Pennsylvania ANG. It was retired on May 7, 2004. NICHOLAS A. VERONICO

During the period that KC-135E 57-1478 *The Guardian* served in the ANG, a squadron would consist of either ten or eleven assigned aircraft. For the most part, when a squadron was deployed, it would do so as a unit, with however many aircraft and crews the mission called for. This was not the case when these squadrons were activated for duty in the First Gulf War. Squadron members and their aircraft could be assigned to any one of the four provisional air refueling wings that had KC-135Es on strength. This applied to the 151st Air Refueling Squadron from Knoxville, Tennessee, which served just over fifteen months on active duty during the war. *The Guardian* was sent to AMARG on June 10, 2009. JIM DUNN

In November 2003, when the 174th Fighter Squadron of the Iowa ANG exchanged its F-16C fighters for KC-135E tankers, they received aircraft from several different ANG squadrons to bring them to full strength. Now becoming a member of the 174th Air Refueling Squadron at Sioux City Gateway Airport, KC-135E 58-0020 *The Veteran* retained the nose art that Donna Pitaro painted when it was a part of the 146th Air Refueling Squadron of the Pennsylvania ANG. It was flown into desert storage on July 24, 2008. NICHOLAS A. VERONICO / JIM DUNN

On rare occasions, a squadron will apply nose art to one of their aircraft to show support for a local or area sports franchise. For the 191st Air Refueling Squadron of the Utah ANG based at Salt Lake City International Airport, the name and logo of their hometown NBA team, the Utah Jazz, would be the final nose art carried by KC-135E 58-0012. After more than twenty-five years with the 191st Air Refueling Squadron in Salt Lake City, 58-0012 *Utah Jazz* would depart for the final time on April 1, 2008. JIM DUNN

Boeing KC-135E Stratotanker 58-0108 *America's King of Aerial Refueling* was delivered to the USAF on October 14, 1959. The plane was last assigned to the 940th Air Refueling Wing at Beale AFB in California. It arrived at AMARG on May 30, 2008. Note the Air Force Reserve and Air Mobility Command shields on the lower fuselage aft of the entry door. RON STRONG / NICHOLAS A. VERONICO

Not much when it comes to nose art, but *Jersey Bounce Jr.*, seen here on KC-135 62-3527, pays tribute to a series of World War II aircraft to wear the name. Consolidated B-24 Liberator bomber 41-23711 of the 93rd Bomb Group was the first to wear it, followed by a pair of B-17s assigned to the 303rd Bomb Group (B-17F 41-24515 *Jersey Bounce* and B-17F 42-29664 *Jersey Bounce Jr.*), another Liberator, and a couple of P-51 Mustangs. The planes were named after a popular song of the time. It was a number-one hit for Benny Goodman (as an instrumental) and was sung by Jimmy Dorsey, who charted as high as number nine with the song. 62-3527 was last operated by the 108th Air Refueling Wing and was flown to storage on February 26, 2008. NICHOLAS A. VERONICO

KC-135E 61-0303 wears the nose art of *Colors of Freedom*, with the title "Never Forget Sept. 11, 2001" below. To the left of the nose art are the markings "In Memory of 'DPQ'—Capt. John P. DePasquale . . . A Father, Husband, Patriot and Friend." This tribute has been seen on a number of tankers: Captain DePasquale must have been someone very special. 61-0303 arrived for storage on May 13, 2008. NICHOLAS A. VERONICO

The nose art of KC-135E 61-0271 *Wings of Freedom* is fading after being retired on May 21, 2007. It is, however, taking on a golden hue. During the Vietnam War, this aircraft was one of seven KC-135As (61-0268, -0270, -0271, -0280, -0303, -0321, and 61-8881) modified to "Combat Lightning" configuration to perform radio-relay duties over the Gulf of Tonkin. These KC-135As were based at Kadena AB, Okinawa, Japan, and relayed information from airborne air controllers in EC-121K Rivet Top and EC-121 Airborne Early Warning and Contol Constellations. The dorsal spine of these aircraft was covered in radio antennas, and the crew typically consisted of two radio operators and two technicians ready to fix any of the electronic boxes in flight. NICHOLAS A. VERONICO

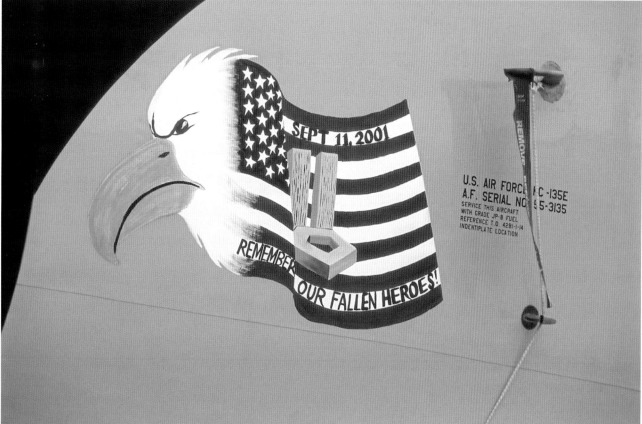

Boeing NKC-135E 55-3135 was retired from the 412th Test Wing at Edwards AFB, California, on September 28, 2004. The starboard side of this aircraft is dotted with viewing ports, and the wing leading edge and engine pylons were painted black to reduce reflections during observations. Also shown is the commemorative nose art worn by 55-3155 during the October 2002 Edwards AFB open house. NICHOLAS A. VERONICO / JIM DUNN

NKC-135A 55-3127 *Thunder Chicken* last served with the 4950th Test Wing at Wright Patterson AFB in Ohio. This aircraft spent the majority of its life configured for airborne radiation measurements. It was flown to storage on August 31, 1992. RON STRONG

KC-135E 59-1445 *When Pigs Fly* last flew with the 108th Air Refueling Wing of the New Jersey ANG. It was retired on July 14, 2009. The unit took up the refueling mission on October 19, 1991, having previously flown the F-105B Thunderchief. The unit now flies the KC-135R. RON STRONG

The C-9A Nightingale was ordered by the USAF to perform the specialized aeromedical evacuation mission. Based on the commercial Douglas DC-9-32CF, the Nightingale is able to carry either forty litter patients or forty ambulatory patients. Since the first of twenty-one aircraft began service in August 1968, these aircraft have flown missions around the world, with C-9A 71-0875 flying the first Nightingale mission into the People's Republic of China on March 27, 1979. Honored with the *Let's Roll* nose art by its final unit, the 30th Airlift Squadron of the 374th Airlift Wing at Yokota AB, Japan, C-9A 71-0875 was flown into retirement on September 4, 2003. JIM DUNN

After arriving at AMARG on March 17, 2004, this is all that remains of KC-135E 55-3141 *Pride of Siouxland*. This tanker, the twenty-fourth KC-135 built by Boeing, served for nearly fifty years, with its name being given by its final unit, the 174th Aerial Refueling Squadron of the Iowa ANG at Sioux City. Prior to serving with the 174th, the aircraft had a long career with the 116th Air Refueling Squadron of the Washington ANG, based at Fairchild AFB. After 55-3141 was retired, the 185th Air Refueling Wing christened 58-0080 *Pride of Siouxland*, which was retired on May 6, 2008. NICHOLAS A. VERONICO / JIM DUNN

Independence Hall, the American flag, and the Liberty Bell adorn the nose of KC-135E 57-2604 *Liberty Belle*. This mural was painted by Donna Pitaro for the 171st Air Refueling Wing of the Pennsylvania ANG. The Stratotanker was flown to AMARG on August 26, 2008. NICHOLAS A. VERONICO

Six giant Lockheed C-5As fill a parking row on the east side of AMARG. Closest to the camera is C-5A 69-0008, wearing the nose art of *The Intimidator* from the 105th Airlift Wing at Stewart ANG Base in Newburgh, New York. It arrived at AMARG on May 3, 2012. Next in line is 69-0003 from the 445th Airlift Wing of Wright-Patterson AFB, Ohio. 69-0003 was flown to AMARG on April 11, 2012. NICHOLAS A. VERONICO

Lockheed C-5A 70-0457 was the first Galaxy received by the 445th Airlift Wing in 2006. The unit had been flying the C-141, and 70-0457's retirement on January 31, 2012, marked the aircraft's replacement with the C-17 Globemaster III. 70-0457 wears a map of the state of Ohio and a tribute to the City of Fairborn, where the Wright Brothers began their work to perfect the heavier-than-air aeroplane. NICHOLAS A. VERONICO

The largest aircraft type stored in AMARG is the Lockheed C-5A Galaxy. Last
assigned to the 137th Airlift Squadron of the New York ANG, C-5A 67-0173
acquired the name *Hudson Howler* for the distinctive howl from its four General
Electric TF39-GE-1C engines. Based in the Hudson Valley at Stewart ANGB, only
sixty miles north of New York City, the unit had close ties to those agencies that
paid a high price in the attacks of September 11, 2001. Outlined by a map of
New York, 67-0173 also carries a special salute to four of the hardest hit emergency
responder units (opposite, bottom). *Hudson Howler* departed for the desert on
October 13, 2004, and in 2012, the 137th Airlift Squadron of the 105th Airlift
Wing completed its transition from the C-5A to the C-17A. JIM DUNN

C-5A 67-0174 was originally delivered to the U.S. Air Force on March 10, 1970. It is from the 137th Airlift Squadron of the 105th Airlift Wing and wears the nose art of *Legend of Sleepy Hollow*. This Galaxy arrived at AMARG on June 14, 2005. RON STRONG

Close-up view of the nose art on C-5A 69-0008 *The Intimidator,* featuring the Tazmanian Devil. Application of the full serial number over the nose art was done at AMARG shortly after the Galaxy arrived. NICHOLAS A. VERONICO

C-5A 70-0459 was christened *Spirit of Erma* in honor of West Virginia Sen. Robert C. Byrd's wife. When many senators were pushing to get new C-17s for the airlift wings in their states, Byrd instead moved to bring the C-5 to the 167th Airlift Wing of the West Virginia ANG because he knew it would bring more jobs to the region around Martinsburg. 70-0459 arrived at AMARG on March 25, 2011. Note the sectioned B-52 to the right under the Galaxy's nose. NICHOLAS A. VERONICO

Based on the C-130H version of the Lockheed Hercules, the National Science Foundation ordered six ski-equipped LC-130R aircraft to provide additional support to Operation Deep Freeze in Antarctica. Operated by the Navy and assigned to VXE-6 at NAS Quonset Point, Rhode Island, LC-130R Buno 159130 *Chilly* flew these support missions from 1974 until its retirement on March 8, 1999. *Chilly* also carried the title *Spirit of Willy Field* in honor of Williams Field, located near McMurdo Station, where it was based when operating in Antarctica. The Deep Freeze support missions were reassigned to the 139th Airlift Squadron of the New York ANG in 1998. JIM DUNN

In January 1955, the Navy established VX-6 at
NAS Patuxent River, Maryland, to begin support
missions for Operation Deep Freeze, followed
by an order for four ski-equipped Hercules first
designated as UV-1Ls, then, in 1962, as KC-
130Fs. Among them was LC-130F Buno 148319
Pride of McMurdo, which served from 1959 until
its retirement on March 10, 1999. While it had a
long service record, this Hercules with Betty
Boop for nose art did not go unscathed. During
1975–76, the ice runway at Dome C, a 10,607-
foot-high Antarctic plateau, was littered with the
wrecks of three LC-130Fs, including Buno
148319, damaged on a takeoff run. Both outer
wings, along with both outboard engines, had to
be replaced. In time, all three aircraft flew
again, and Betty Boop would ride along on
many more successful flights. JIM DUNN

LC-130F Buno 148321 from VXE-6 wears the name *Phoenix* and a rendering of the mythical bird said to have risen from the ashes of its predecessor. This Hercules was making a JATO takeoff on December 17, 1971, when two JATO bottles came off the front fuselage and struck the number-two engine and propeller, causing the propeller to depart the aircraft. Debris from the impact damaged the number-one propeller, and the aircraft dropped fifty feet back to the snow and ice. None of the ten crew members was seriously injured, and they were rescued four days later when the weather cleared. Buno 148321 was abandoned on the ice and eventually was buried to almost the top of the tail. In 1986, work to recover the Hercules began. It was dug out, the engines and propellers were sent for overhaul, and the aircraft weas reassembled. It was flown off the ice on January 10, 1988, and returned to service after overhaul. It was finally retired to the warmth of the Arizona desert on March 29, 1999. NICHOLAS A. VERONICO

Lockheed DC-130A 57-0497 is a drone controller and was used to launch BQM-34 and BQM-74 target drones from pylons under the outer wings. When this Hercules was retired, arriving at AMARG on June 27, 2007, it was the oldest C-130 in the U.S. military. It now resides in a place on honor on AMARG's Celebrity Row. NICHOLAS A. VERONICO

Called by many the "Purple Heart Herc," C-130E 63-7865 came to AMARG from the 86th Airlift Wing, Ramstein Air Base, Germany, on June 9, 2008, when the unit began receiving new C-130Js. During the Vietnam War, this Hercules earned an honorary Purple Heart for damage it sustained on June 1, 1972, at Kontum Air Base. One mortar round damaged the number-three engine, which was replaced but would not start, so the aircraft took off under heavy fire on three engines. Unable to fly higher than 1,000 feet, 63-7865 was an easy target for gunners on the ground. The plane set down at Pleiku Air Base, where it was determined that it would need two new wings as well as four new engines and new propellers. After repairs were made, 63-7865 continued to serve the Air Force through Operations Desert Storm and Iraqi Freedom, and it now resides on AMARG's Celebrity Row, where visitors can see it on the daily tours. NICHOLAS A. VERONICO

Named for the Norse god of poetry and music, C-130H 68-10957 *Brage* arrived at AMARG on December 15, 2008, after being withdrawn from use with nearly forty years of service to the Royal Norwegian Air Force. The last of six C-130s ordered by Norway and delivered in June 1969, *Brage* spent its entire service with No. 335 Squadron of 135 Air Wing at Gardermoen Air Station at the Oslo International Airport. These six Royal Norwegian Air Force C-130s had completed 132,000 flight hours without a major mishap. They were replaced in 2008 by four C-130Js that were given the names of goddesses who were the wives of the gods named on the C-130Hs. JIM DUNN

In the years since the end of World War II, a number of USAF aircraft have worn copies of the famous nose art that adorned the B-17F *Memphis Belle*. Seen here in a private storage yard in Tucson, C-130A 57-0463 has the image incorporated into the emblem of the 164th Tactical Airlift Group of the Tennessee ANG, in which it last served. Assigned to the 155th Tactical Airlift Squadron at Memphis International Airport, the aircraft was retired for the second and final time in 1991, with a total of 14,825.8 hours in its log book. This *Memphis Belle* was sold in 1996 to a private dealer and removed from the then Aircraft Maintenance and Regeneration Center (AMARC). JIM DUNN

On the tails of most USAF active-duty aircraft are the common points of identification: American flag, the major command emblem, and tail code. With C-130E 63-7821, an additional emblem shows the *Samurai* of the 374th Airlift Wing at Yokota AB, Japan, to which it was assigned. Within the wing, it was assigned to the 36th Airlift Squadron, with the aircraft also denoted as representing the 374th Operations Group of the wing. The operations group is the next organization under the wing and is directly in charge of the squadrons. Only one aircraft within the wing is normally designated to carry the operations group markings. *Samurai* was flown back to the states and retired on December 15, 2006. JIM DUNN

After nearly forty years of service, EC-130E 62-1836 made its final trip to AMARG on September 29, 2009, on the end of a tow bar. Until 2002, it had served its primary mission as an airborne battlefield command control center (ABCCC) in combat zones from Vietnam to the Balkans. Its last service in an ABCCC role was with the 42nd Airborne Command & Control Squadron at Davis-Monthan AFB, with a final seven-year tour at Davis-Monthan in the 79th Rescue Squadron, which is assigned to the 563rd Rescue Group, which in turn is under the "Flying Tigers" of the 23rd Wing at Moody AFB, Georgia. It is because of that connection to the Flying Tigers that the aircraft wears the famous shark mouth. JIM DUNN

Last assigned to United States Air Forces Europe with the 37th Airlift Squadron of the 86th Airlift Wing at Ramstein AB, Germany, C-130E 64-18240 carries the *Let's Roll* nose art adopted by the USAF after the attacks of September 11, 2001. The phrase was the rallying last words of Todd Beamer, a passenger on United Airlines Flight 93 who helped foil the terrorists from crashing the airliner into the United States Capitol. In the USAF, most commands allow the *Let's Roll* nose art on one aircraft in each wing, with C-130E 64-18240 being given that honor in the 86th Airlift Wing until its retirement on August 20, 2009. JIM DUNN

Lockheed KC-130F wears the tail and fuselage codes QD-573 representing its last operator, Marine Air Refueling and Transport Squadron 152 (VMGR-152) stationed at MCAS Iwakuni, Japan. The aircraft commander listed on the nose, Lt. Col. D. C. Neely, was commander of the U.S. Navy Flight Demonstration's transport, known as *Fat Albert*, from 1998 to 2000. NICHOLAS A. VERONICO

NOSE ART ARTISTS: AN EXCLUSIVE CLUB

Nose art as we know it today gained popularity on the sides of aircraft in every theater of World War II. The fuselages of bombers—B-17s, B-24s, and B-29s—made for especially great canvases while the fighters of the day—P-39s, P-40s, P-47s, and P-51s—were somewhat more sedate but no less elaborate.

Although their creations are well known, the majority of the artists did not receive recognition outside their squadrons or wings until long after the conclusion of hostilities. Cpl. Anthony "Tony" Starcer was responsible for 124 nose art paintings on 91st Bomb Group aircraft while stationed in England, but it was his work on *Memphis Belle* that garnered him some recognition during the war. It wasn't until the early 1970s, when the warbird and World War II history movement took hold, that historians began to research nose art and those who created it.

During the 1980s the tradition of nose art began to make its return on the sides of Strategic Air Command B-52s and KC-135 tankers. Among those painting SAC heavies was M/Sgt. Shayne Meder, who was decorating 410th Bombardment Wing aircraft at K. I. Sawyer AFB in Michigan. Meder painted B-52Hs *Stratofortress Rex* (60-0048), *Shack Rabbit* (61-0025), *Rocky* (60-0026), *American Eagle* (61-0015), and *Nightstalker* (61-0020).

In 1990 Meder was transferred to Castle AFB in California, home of the 93rd Bomb Wing. When the base closed in 1995, Meder retired and ran the restoration shops at the Castle Air Museum and later the March Field Museum in California. In addition to restoring the museum's aircraft, Meder also painted a number of operational aircraft at March Field. After eight years at the museum, Meder joined the Wings and Rotors Air Museum in 2003, located at the French Valley Airport in Murrieta, California. Here she has devoted her talents to restoring the Rotors and Wings Museum's collection and painting more than thirty U.S. Navy CAG-bird (Commander, Air Group) H-60 helicopters at nearby NAS North Island.

Derrel Fleener had been in the Air Force, and in the late 1980s was executive director of the Silver Wings Aviation Museum at Mather AFB, outside Sacramento. His association with nose art painting came about rather simply: "The people from the 320th Bomb Wing knew that I was an artist, and they just asked me if I'd paint some of the aircraft. The crews pretty much left everything up to me. They were just really glad to get someone to do it, so they just let it roll," Fleener said.

During World War II, three B-17s and a pair of B-24s were called *Shack Rabbit*. Forty years later, Shayne Meder updated the nose art of *Shack Rabbit* on B-52H 61-0025 with a stylized Jessica Rabbit character. In her spare time today, Meder paints the tails of H-60 helicopters at Naval Air Station North Island in San Diego. SHAYNE MEDER

Artist Derrel Fleener details his nose art painting of *Strangelove*, a B-52G (58-0234) from the 320th Bomb Wing based at Mather Field outside Sacramento. Fleener's adaptation of Slim Pickens riding the nuclear bomb from the movie *Dr. Strangelove* was a favorite of the 320th. JIM DUNN

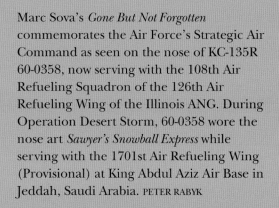

Marc Sova's *Gone But Not Forgotten* commemorates the Air Force's Strategic Air Command as seen on the nose of KC-135R 60-0358, now serving with the 108th Air Refueling Squadron of the 126th Air Refueling Wing of the Illinois ANG. During Operation Desert Storm, 60-0358 wore the nose art *Sawyer's Snowball Express* while serving with the 1701st Air Refueling Wing (Provisional) at King Abdul Aziz Air Base in Jeddah, Saudi Arabia. PETER RABYK

During his time painting aircraft for the 320th Bomb Wing, Fleener painted eight B-52Gs, including *Strangelove* (58-0234), *Yossarian's Question* (59-2585), *City of Sacramento* (57-6469), and *Son of Kilroy* (58-0230). His nose art for B-52G *Express Delivery* (57-6489) is preserved at the National Museum of the U.S. Air Force in Dayton, Ohio.

Fleener's most widely recognized painting is *Old Soldier*, on B-52G 58-0178. This painting shows Gen. Douglas MacArthur chewing on his trademark corncob pipe with the words "Old Soldier" fading off into the distance. This is a quote from MacArthur's famous line that "Old soldiers never die, they just fade away." In addition, Fleener painted a pair of KC-135s, including KC-135E *Foxy Lady* (55-3145). There were complaints that the lady was too foxy, and Fleener subsequently repainted the nose art as *Mallard 1*.

Of his artwork, Fleener said: "It was a fun thing and I was really happy to do it. It was like recapturing a little bit of history. I was thinking that of all the things that I have done, I might be best known for that little period of time when I painted those B-52s."

When the F-105 Thunderchief and the A-7 Corsair II went to the Virginia ANG, they came under the brush of Sgt. Bernard "Beetle" Bailey. Through the years, Bailey transformed thirty-one F-105s and twenty-nine A-7s from nameless flying machines to planes with their own personalities.

In 1995, Steve Barba was transferred to the 37th Maintenance Squadron at Ellsworth AFB in South Dakota. When the squadron's original nose artist was transferred out, Barba was given "a try." His art was well received, and the majority of the B-1B Lancer bombers were decorated by Barba from then on. He counts forty-nine B-1B Lancers to his credit, including *Intimidator* (85-0085), *Fury 1* (86-0128), *Wolf Pack* (86-0096), and *Dakota Queen* (86-0139), a tribute to South Dakota senator and World War II B-24 pilot George S. McGovern. Today Barba is retired and continues to paint in South Dakota.

Within days of the September 11, 2001, terrorist attacks on the United States, southern Illinois–based artist Marc Sova of Sova Studios was contacted to paint a patriotic, commemorative nose art piece on KC-135E 59-1487. *United in Memory: September 11, 2001* features the sun rising over planet earth, a bald eagle, and the Pentagon in remembrance of those who perished on American Airlines Flight 77 and inside the Pentagon.

Sova began his art career as a teenager, airbrushing designs on T-shirts, cars, and trucks. This carried him through art school, where he honed his craft and earned a fine arts degree. His teenage years gave him a

great amount of experience in painting on metal. "I have a technique where I use sort of a pattern—like a pounce pattern, which is an old, old method that goes all the way back to frescos and the Renaissance, where an artist pokes holes in paper and then they pounce powdered charcoal through it to give an outline," said Sova. "I have a little bit of a different take on the pounce technique that I kind of invented. I use a special type of cloth that I draw the design on in my studio. Then I trace over that design with my airbrush, and it goes through the cloth. Most of the nose art paintings that use my modified pounce technique are relatively freehand. The ones that get more involved with a lot of lettering and a lot of detail, sometimes I have stencils. I design it all in the computer, making vector files, and I send them off to a sign shop buddy who cuts vinyl stencils for me. It's a little bit of a different technique on a few of them, but all involve mostly airbrush and spray guns. I don't really do a lot of hand brushing."

Sova's art has made it around the world, and some have flown into the boneyard, including KC-135Es *Belleville Bill* (58-0068), *American Made* (58-0024), *Flying Dog* (57-1480), *Fill 'Er Up Doc* (57-1497), and *Easyrider* (58-0003).

If Tony Starcer was the king of nose art in World War II (as measured by the estimated 124 aircraft he painted), then Donna Pitaro is today's reigning queen. The Pittsburgh-area artist is responsible for seventy-five flying canvases on aircraft with the 171st AW and the 911th Airlift Wing, both components of the Pennsylvania ANG. "In 1998, the 171st AW was looking for an artist to paint nose art on the unit's KC-135s. At the suggestion of my brother-in-law, I did one, and they loved it," Pitaro said. "I have been privileged and honored to paint these aircraft and to have done it for so long."

Pitaro credits the return of nose art on the 171st Air Wing's aircraft to Col. Tom Hess. He has the crew chiefs and the men and women of the unit come up with the theme and what they would like to see. They then get the concept approved by higher headquarters. Once approved, Pitaro takes the idea and creates a painting using that guidance. "Each crew chief has a little personal touch that they add to their plane's nose art. They'll ask me on the side, 'Hey, can you put in. . . .' One crew chief really liked Rolling Rock beer, so we added the horse from the brewery's logo. Crew chief Lenny Flowers's nickname was 'Rosebud,' so there's a rosebud in his plane's nose art. When I did the *Pirate Ship*, that crew chief was really into NASCAR. So we put the number of his favorite driver into the painting. But I think the coolest thing we do at the 171st is we hide— kind of like *Where's Waldo?*—a Strategic Air Command

Artist Donna Pitaro with KC-135T *Generations of Pride* (58-0054), which commemorates the aircraft flown by the 171st Air Refueling Wing and its antecedent units. Note the Strategic Air Command mailed fist on the arm of the Keystone Cop at the top of the nose art. (This KC-135 was the first aircraft to refuel an SR-71.) SHAWN MONK

KC-135E 57-1509 wears the Donna Pitaro nose art *Spirit of Pittsburgh*. The painting features the Omnichron, a little alien creature receiving fuel that was developed during World War II, along with Pittsburgh's waterfront and skyline. Note the line of tankers in storage in the background. NICHOLAS A. VERONICO

mailed fist grasping lightning bolts in every single nose art." Pitaro says you have to look hard, but they are there. Some are as small as a quarter while others might be the size of a hand.

"I use acrylic enamel paint with a fast reducer that dries pretty quickly," Pitaro said. "The planes have to be out of the hangar in so many days, and luckily, I can paint pretty fast. So there hasn't usually been a problem. I work right in the hangar with the crews. But a couple of times, we had to pull the plane out, and I have to work outside, which was a nightmare, but most of the time I'm inside."

The art has covered a wide range of subjects. "We've done all kind of themes. We've done patriotic themes. We've done cities, Pittsburgh themes, and we've done a lot of sports themes," Pitaro said. "We had the Pittsburgh Penguins hockey team–themed nose art that we did a year and a half ago. When that painting was done, all of the Penguins players came out and signed the aircraft. We've done historic pieces which incorporate the Keystone Lady, a Pennsylvania historic symbol. We've also done something to commemorate different tragedies like September 11th. We did a couple of nose arts to remember that event. On the lighter side, we've done Warner Brothers nose art where we had to get copyright permission from the studio. We did the Tasmanian Devil and Yosemite Sam, both of which were very popular."

On the C-130s of the 911th Airlift Wing, Pitaro has painted a September 11 tribute in *We have not forgotten* and, to commemorate all of the men and women who have served our nation, *Freedom isn't free*. This C-130's nose art depicts a rifle in the ground with empty boots

and a helmet to signify a fallen comrade. Another was *Flight 93: American Heroes* that showed planes ascending into the sky with an eagle coming out of the clouds. "It was pretty powerful," she said.

Nose art builds esprit de corps, gives an aircraft a visual personality, and is great to look at. Those who have taken a unit's concept and painted their interpretation on the nose panels of an aircraft are a privileged few, members of an exclusive club. Each artist believes that painting nose art in tribute to our nation's men and women in uniform is an honor and a privilege.

Seen at Brown Field, San Diego, during the February 2011 celebration of the 100th anniversary of naval aviation, C-130H 78-0812 from the 758th AS, 911th AW, based in Pittsburgh, carries Donna Pitaro's *Freedom Isn't Free* nose art in honor of all Persian Gulf War veterans. JIM DUNN

Prodded by its experience with Iraqi Scud missiles during the First Gulf War, the Air Force wanted a laser-equipped Boeing 747 that could seek and destroy a missile from beyond a hostile country's borders within ten seconds. Boeing provided the aircraft, Northrop Grumman the laser, and Lockheed Martin the fire-control system and nose turret to produce the YAL-1 Airborne Laser Test Bed able to fire a one-megawatt chemical oxygen iodine laser (COIL). On February 2, 2010, the YAL-1 destroyed a solid-fuel rocket and, nine days later, destroyed a sea-launched, liquid-fuel ballistic missile, but it later fell victim to budget cuts. On February 14, 2012, the YAL-1 made its last flight, from its home at Edwards AFB to AMARG, where the flying test bed was preserved and put into the storage. The plane had flown 100 to 110 missions, acquiring 250 cycles and more than 900 flight hours. NICHOLAS A. VERONICO

Close-up view of the YAL-1 Airborne Laser Test Bed shows the laser turret, windscreen, and other openings covered with spraylat preservative. The protrusion on top of the fuselage is a Low Altitude Navigation and Targeting Infrared for Night (LANTIRN) targeting pod. It has been reported that after the YAL-1 is dismantled, the nose turret will be removed and sent to the National Museum of the U.S. Air Force for eventual display. NICHOLAS A. VERONICO

Seven missile tracking marks and two kill marks were painted under the cockpit windows on both sides of the aircraft. NICHOLAS A. VERONICO

The logos of the agencies participating in the Airborne Laser Test Bed on the upper sides of the YAL-1's fuselage are the Air Combat Command, Air Force Materiel Command, and Missile Defense Agency. NICHOLAS A. VERONICO

Although there's a canopy reflection across the front of the aircraft in this photo, it does show Boeing KC-135E 63-8050 *Big Crow II*, which was flown as a target for the Airborne Laser Test Bed. The white shape on the forward fuselage simulates a missile while the white light aft the missile markings shows where an infrared hot spot would be located during testing. The YAL-1's onboard infrared sensors would detect the missile's heat signature and then begin the targeting sequence by firing a low-energy targeting laser to measure atmospheric conditions. This information would be computed and fed to the laser, which would destroy the target. NORTHROP GRUMMAN

Right side markings on NKC-135E 63-8050 *Big Crow II*. Both target NKC-135Es were operated by the 452nd FLTS Det.2 from Kirtland AFB, New Mexico, part of the Air Force Materiel Command at Edwards AFB under that base's 412th Test Wing. NICHOLAS A. VERONICO

Both sides of NKC-135E 55-3132 *Big Crow I* in storage at AMARG. *Big Crow I* and *Big Crow II* both arrived at AMARG on September 16, 2009. NICHOLAS A. VERONICO

The U.S. Missile Defense Agency used this McDonnell-Douglas DC-10-10 (msn 46524, N910SF, ex-American Airlines N124AA) as its Widebody Airborne Sensor Platform (WASP) in the development of a ballistic missile detection system. The DC-10 was used for various tests by Hughes Aircraft Co., Raytheon, and the U.S. Air Force. In the late 1990s, this aircraft wore the name *Sweet Judy* under the pilot's window. NICHOLAS A. VERONICO

The Open Skies Treaty, signed March 24, 1992, enables nations to fly unarmed reconnaissance flights to gather military information about another Open Skies Treaty state. OC-135B 61-2674 was part of the U.S. fleet of aircraft enforcing the treaty. Flights are typically conducted with little notice in an effort to see as much as possible. 61-2674 was last operated by the 55th Wing at Offutt AFB, Nebraska, and arrived at AMARG for storage on August 21, 1997. NICHOLAS A. VERONICO

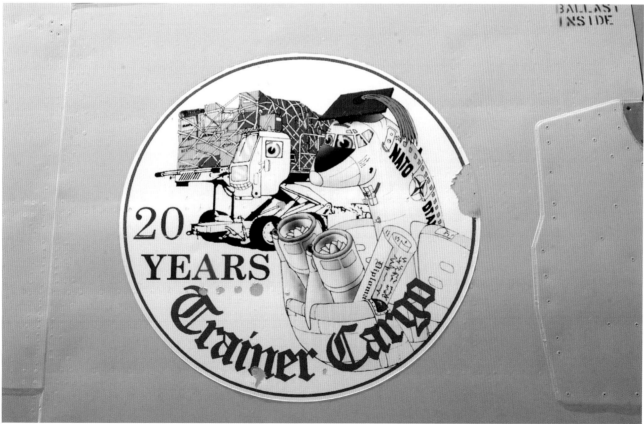

Boeing 707-307C (msn 20000) was delivered to the West German Air Force as 10+04 in November 1968. Twenty years later, in July 1998, the aircraft was transferred to NATO as LX N20000. The jet wears the colors of NATO and was used as a staff transport and to keep NATO E-3A Sentry pilots current. NICHOLAS A. VERONICO

Originally built to be launched from the backs of modified A-11 Blackbirds, the D-21 drone was eventually launched from the wing pylons of B-52s. Although successful, the D-21s suffered many teething troubles and the Mach 3+ drone was shelved. Many considered it far ahead of its time. Most of the seventeen D-21 drones delivered to AMARG have been farmed out to museums while a couple remain in storage for eventual display. NICHOLAS A. VERONICO

Former United DC-8-54AF (msn 45881, N8048U) was delivered to the airline in 1966. The carrier parked the plane in November 1984 and subsequently sold it to the U.S. Navy, which converted it to EC-24A Buno 163050 in June 1987. The plane was used as an aggressor, simulating various hostile radars. NICHOLAS A. VERONICO

Grumman E-2C Hawkeye airborne early-warning aircraft Buno 161783 was the VAW-77 Night Wolves squadron commander's aircraft. The squadron was shore-based at Joint Reserve Base New Orleans but was disestablished due to budget cuts in February 2013. Buno 161783 arrived for storage on March 10, 2005. NICHOLAS A. VERONICO

E-2C 163024 from Carrier Airborne Early Warning Squadron One Two Six (VAW-126, "The Seahawks") is one of twenty-five Hawkeyes in storage at AMARG. In December 2002, VAW-126 sailed aboard USS *Harry S. Truman* to support forces in Operation Iraqi Freedom. The unit set a record of 100 sorties in 445 hours before returning to Norfolk in May 2003. Buno 163024 wears the nose art *Give 'Em Hell!* and thirty-four electronic mission marks from Iraqi Freedom. This aircraft arrived at AMARG for storage on July 11, 2003, shortly after returning home. Its radome has been removed to provide parts for other aircraft flying with the fleet. RON STRONG

E-2C Buno 161345 last served with the Naval Air Warfare Center–Aircraft Division (NAWC-AD), which has facilities at Joint Base McGuire-Dix-Lakehurst in New Jersey, NAS Patuxent River in Maryland, and Orlando in Florida. NAWC-AD provides research, test, engineering, and evaluation for all aviation products in the Navy and Marine Corps throughout their lifecycles. This aircraft was sent to storage on September 21, 1993. RON STRONG

The E-2C has five crew members, two flying and three systems operators, who provide command-and-control and surface-surveillance information to fleet commanders. The twenty-four-foot-diameter radome above the fuselage houses the AN/APS-145 search radar. E-2C Buno 164110 last flew with Carrier Airborne Command and Control Squadron 120 (VAW-120, "The Greyhawks"), the sole E-2 training squadron for the U.S. Navy. Notice the eight scimitar-shaped propeller blades on this recent AMARG arrival. NICHOLAS A. VERONICO

Highly modified Lockheed NP-3D Orion Buno 150499 has been fitted with Extended Area Test System (EATS) radar ahead of the vertical stabilizer. The plane was last used by VX-9 at China Lake and VX-30 at Point Mugu for range control and test data collection. Retired to AMARG on April 13, 2006, and now a resident of Celebrity Row.
NICHOLAS A. VERONICO

Since its arrival on October 2, 2009, Grumman EA-6B Prowler Buno 158030 went directly to parts-reclamation storage. The nose radome, engines, and cowlings have been returned to the fleet to keep other electronic warfare Prowlers in the air. NICHOLAS A. VERONICO

Lockheed ES-3A from Fleet Air Reconnaissance Squadron Five (VQ-5, "The Sea Shadows") arrived at AMARG only two days after the squadron was disestablished on June 5, 1999. The electronic-reconnaissance version of the S-3, the ES-3A, was phased out in favor of the land-based EP-3E Aries II. NICHOLAS A. VERONICO

Lockheed S-3B Viking Buno 158861 flew with Sea Control Squadron 30 (VS-30, "The Diamond Cutters") in support of Operation Iraqi Freedom from the decks of the USS *John F. Kennedy* (CV-67). The plane wears the motto "Defending Freedom to the Very Last Day." When the squadron returned to NAS Jacksonville, Buno 158861 was flown into retirement on January 3, 2005, as the unit began the draw-down process. VS-30 was disestablished on December 9, 2005. RON STRONG

Lockheed S-3B Viking Buno 159390 *Bonesaw* also flew with VS-30 and arrived on January 3, 2005. In addition to the shark mouth on the nose, the tail featured a Florida license plate that read "Got Gas." RON STRONG

The Beech T-34 Mentor has been serving the U.S. military as a trainer since the early 1950s. The turboprop-powered T-34C, rows of which are seen here, is now being replaced by the more modern T-6 Texan II trainer.
NICHOLAS A. VERONICO

Sikorsky MH-53E Sea Dragon Buno 162516 from Helicopter Combat Support Squadron Four (HC-4) was shore-based at NAS Sigonella on Sicily until its retirement on April 19, 2004. The squadron name, "Black Stallions," is painted on the landing-gear sponson. RON STRONG

Helicopter Anti-Submarine Squadron Light 42 (HSL-42) transitioned from the SH-60B to the MH-60R Sea Hawk helicopter in spring 2013. With the transition comes a new unit name: Helicopter Maritime Strike Squadron 72 (HSM-72). SH-60B Buno 162111 arrived at AMARG on January 13, 2011. NICHOLAS A. VERONICO

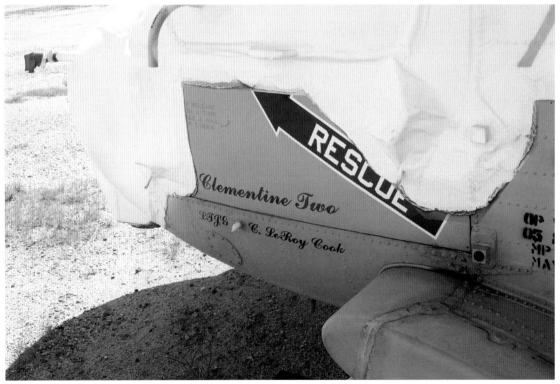

Sikorsky SH-60F Buno 164073 came to AMARG from the HS-10 "Warhawks" on December 6, 2011. The helicopter was painted in a Medal of Honor tribute to Lt. j.g. Clyde Everett Lassen, who flew with Helicopter Support Squadron 7, Detachment 104, on board the destroyer USS *Preble* (DLG-15) in the waters off Vietnam. Lassen and his crew flew their UH-2 Seasprite helicopter deep into enemy-held territory to rescue a pair of downed pilots at night under withering fire. During the rescue, while hovering between two trees, his main rotor struck one of them, but Lassen recovered, picked up both pilots, and limped to a destroyer offshore, landing with only five minutes of fuel left. Lassen was awarded the nation's highest honor by Lyndon B. Johnson, becoming the first naval aviator awarded the Medal of Honor in the Vietnam War. He passed away in 1994, and the paint scheme on Buno 164073 is a fitting tribute to this aviator. NICHOLAS A. VERONICO

The crew of Clementine Two that rescued the two downed Phantom jet pilots in Vietnam on June 19, 1968. Clockwise from the top left: Pilot Lt. j.g. Clyde Lassen, Co-pilot Lt. j.g. LeRoy Cook, gunners ADJ3 Don West and AE2 Bruce Dallas.

Congressional Medal of Honor
Clyde Everett Lassen

Lieutenant, U.S. Navy, Helicopter Support Squadron 7, Detachment 104, embarked in U.S.S. Preble (DLG-15) Republic of Vietnam, 19 June 1968

For conspicuous gallantry and intrepidity at the risk of his life above and beyond the call of duty as pilot and aircraft commander of a search and rescue helicopter, attached to Helicopter Support Squadron 7, during operations against enemy forces in North Vietnam. Launched shortly after midnight to attempt the rescue of 2 downed aviators. Lt. J.G Lassen skillfully piloted his aircraft over unknown and hostile terrain to a steep, tree-covered hill on which the survivors had been located. Although enemy fire was being directed at the helicopter, he initially landed in a clear area near the base of the hill, but due to the dense undergrowth, the survivors could not reach the helicopter. With the aid of flare illumination, Lt. Lassen successfully accomplished a hover between 2 trees at the survivors' position. Illumination was abruptly lost as the last of the flares were expended, and the helicopter collided with a tree, commencing a sharp descent. Expertly righting his aircraft and maneuvering clear, Lt. Lassen remained in the area, determined to make another rescue attempt, and encouraged the downed aviators while awaiting resumption of flare illumination. After another unsuccessful, illuminated rescue attempt and with his fuel dangerously low and his aircraft significantly damaged, he launched again and commenced another approach in the face of the continuing enemy opposition. When flare illumination was again lost, Lt. Lassen, fully aware of the dangers in clearly revealing his position to the enemy, turned on his landing lights and completed the landing. On this attempt, the survivors were able to make their way to the helicopter. In route to the coast he encountered and successfully evaded additional hostile antiaircraft fire and, with fuel for only minutes of flight remaining, landed safely aboard U.S.S. Jouett (DLG-29). Lt. Lassen's extraordinary heroism at the risk of his life, above and beyond the call of duty, are in keeping with the highest traditions of the military service and reflect great credit upon himself, his unit, and the U.S. Navy.   To the crew we dedicate this aircraft.

LTJG LeRoy Cook received the Navy Cross; ADJ3 Don West and AE2 Bruce Dallas received the Silver Star

RESERVOIR DOG

DON'T WORRY,
ITS GOOD...
ENOUGH.

CREWCHIEF
LCPL
TYLER DEAN
LENEXA KS

1ST MECH
LCPL JON EVERY
FORT WORTH TX

CH-46E Buno 157655 *Reservoir Dog* was last stationed with Marine Medium Helicopter Squadron 163 (HMM-163) at MCAS Miramar in California. It arrived for storage on May 23, 2006, and was struck off the Navy's inventory on July 19, 2006. NICHOLAS A. VERONICO

These MiG-17s and MiG-21s were secretly imported to the United States in the mid-1980s and used in a classified program known as Constant Peg and with the Defense Test and Evalutaion Support Agency at Kirtland AFB in New Mexico. Highly trained U.S. pilots flew the MiGs in engagements with Air Force, Navy, and Marine Corps pilots to give them firsthand exposure to MiGs and Soviet tactics. NICHOLAS A. VERONICO

WB-57F 63-13295 was flown into storage on July 26, 1972. Nearly forty years later, the Canberra was pulled out of storage and returned to service with NASA (NASA 927) in June 2011. NICHOLAS A. VERONICO

WB-57F 63-13290 last flew with the 58th Weather Reconnaissance Squadron at Kirtland AFB, New Mexico. The Martin B-57 was the American license-built version of the British English Electric Canberra bomber and had the engine mounted right through the wing. The WB-57F was a high-altitude reconnaissance conversion of the B-57B fitted with an enlarged 122-foot wing. Seventeen were so modified. NICHOLAS A. VERONICO

AC-130A 55-0029 *Midnight Express* saw extensive service in Vietnam flying support missions from Ubon Royal Thai Air Force Base in Thailand. It last saw service with the 711th Special Operations Squadron of the 919th Special Operations Group out of Duke Field, Florida. With that unit, it participated in Operation Just Cause in Panama and Operation Desert Storm. Notice the targeting radar and gun ports in the forward fuselage. *Midnight Express* was flown to storage on November 15, 1994. NICHOLAS A. VERONICO

APPENDIX: AMARG AND PIMA AIR & SPACE MUSEUM

Tours of AMARG are available for the general public through the Pima Air & Space Museum (6000 East Valencia Road, Tucson, Arizona). Tour buses depart the museum's entrance for AMARG Monday through Friday, excluding federal holidays. Cameras are allowed on the one- to one-and-a-half-hour narrated tour, and visitors must remain on the bus at all times.

Reservations are recommended and should be made at least seven days in advance. There is a small charge for the tour, and additional details can be found on the museum's webpage. Everyone over sixteen must present photo identification.

In addition to its AMARG tours, the Pima Air & Space Museum holds one of the most diverse collections of

The Pima Air & Space Museum has an excellent collection of strategic bombers from the pre–World War II B-18 Bolo to the B-52. The museum's B-29 44-70016 *Sentimental Journey* served with the 330th Bomb Group, based on Guam during World War II. NICHOLAS A. VERONICO

military aircraft, many of which were formerly stored at AMARG. The museum was founded in 1966 by the Air Force Association's Tucson chapter, and in October 1969, thirty-five aircraft from the storage facility's Celebrity Row were transferred to the museum to form the basis of the collection. The museum and its collection of seventy-five aircraft formally opened to the public on May 8, 1976.

Today there are more than 275 aircraft in the collection, ranging from World War II–era bombers such as the B-17, B-24, and B-29 to the Century series of fighters (F-101, F-102, F-104, F-105, and F-106), the VC-118 used by Presidents Kennedy and Johnson, and the supersonic B-58 and SR-71. The museum has a snack bar and well-stocked gift shop. All public areas of the facility are handicapped accessible.

The Pima Air & Space Museum opened the Titan Missile Museum twenty-five miles south of Tucson (1580 West Duval Mine Road, Sahuarita, Arizona) in May 1986. Tours of the former Titan II missile in its underground silo show the complex as it was when operated by the U.S. Air Force's 390th Strategic Missile Wing. Visit the museum's website for tour times and prices. Additionally, the Pima Air & Space Museum is the site of The Challenger Learning Center of the Southwest, which opened to the public in March 1999.

Additional information, events, and a listing of Pima Air & Space Museum aircraft can be obtained at www.pimaair.org.

Convair B-36J Peacemaker 52-2827 wears the mid-1950s colors of the 95th Bomb Wing from Biggs AFB, outside El Paso, Texas. The Peacemaker was the last piston-powered bomber in the U.S. Air Force's inventory.
NICHOLAS A. VERONICO

The Pima Air & Space Museum displays a number of B-52G nose art panels that were removed when the bombers were scrapped. Named after the largest city near Castle AFB in California, *City of Merced* adorned B-52G 58-0207. *Hoosier Hot Shot* was worn by B-52G 57-6486, which arrived at AMARG for storage on August 15, 1991, and was cut into five pieces to comply with the START Treaty on October 1, 2001. The nose art of B-52G 58-0236 *Lucky 13* was worn on the right side of the aircraft under the copilot's window; this Stratofortress was flown to storage on October 13, 1992, and sold for scrap on April 29, 1999. NICHOLAS A. VERONICO

BIBLIOGRAPHY AND SUGGESTED READING

Blanchard, Peter, et al. *MASDC: Military Aircraft Storage & Disposition Center.* London: Aviation Press Ltd., 1983.

Bonny, Danny, et al. *AMARC—Aerospace Maintenance & Regeneration Center, Davis-Monthan AFB, Arizona 1982–1997 (MASDC III).* Surrey, England: British Aviation Research Group, 2006.

Causey, Danny, and Gregory Causey. *Denizens of the Desert: AMARC Photographs by Danny Causey.* Springboro, OH: Romance Divine, 2008.

Chinnery, Philip D. *Boneyard Badges: Aircraft and Emblems at Davis-Monthan AFB.* Shrewsbury, England: Airlife, 2000.

———. *Desert Boneyard.* Shrewsbury, England: Airlife, 1987.

———. *50 Years of the Desert Boneyard.* Osceola, WI: Motorbooks International, 1995.

Fryer, Barry, and Martyn Swann. *AMARC—Aerospace Maintenance & Regeneration Center, Davis-Monthan AFB, Arizona 1982–1997 (MASDC II).* London: Aviation Press, 1998.

Fugere, Jerry, and Bob Shane. *Inside AMARC: The Aerospace Maintenance and Regeneration Center, Tucson, Arizona.* St. Paul, MN: MBI Publishing, 2001.

Johnson, Dave. *The Aerospace Maintenance and Regeneration Center.* West Drayton, England: LAAS International, 1995.

Kramer, Adel, and Patrick Hoeveler. *Desert Boneyards: Retired Aircraft Storage Facilities in the U.S.* Atglen, PA: Schiffer Military Publishing, 2010.

Larkins, William T. *Surplus WWII U.S. Aircraft.* Upland, CA: BAC Publishers, 2005.

Scroggins, James Douglas, and Nicholas A. Veronico. *Junkyard Jets.* Minneapolis, MN: Stance and Speed, 2010.

Veronico, Nicholas A. *Blue Angels: A Fly-By History: Sixty Years of Aerial Excellence.* Osceloa, WI: Zenith Press, 2005.

Veronico, Nicholas A., and Jim Dunn. *Giant Cargo Planes.* Osceola, WI: MBI Publishing, 1999.

———. *21st Century U.S. Air Power.* St. Paul, MN: MBI Publishing, 2004.

Veronico, Nicholas A., and Ron Strong. *AMARG: America's Military Aircraft Boneyard.* North Branch, MN: Specialty Press, 2010.

Veronico, Nicholas A., et al. *Military Aircraft Boneyards.* St. Paul, MN: MBI Publishing, 2000.

WEB LINKS

The AMARC Experience: www.amarcexperience.com
Martyn Swann's AMARC website: www.amarc.info
Steve Barba's nose art: www.thunderbolt-gallery.com
Phil Smith's nose art: www.philsmith.us
Marc Sova's nose art: www.sovastudios.com

ACKNOWLEDGMENTS

Having the opportunity to see America's military aircraft in storage is a privilege, one the authors are very grateful for. We owe a debt of gratitude to the command of the 309th AMARG and to the men and women who work day in and day out to harvest the parts and preserve the aircraft. Thank you.

In addition, many photographers, aviation enthusiasts, and historians have generously given time, images, and access to their collections to make this volume possible. A debt of gratitude is owed to Ian Abbott, Steve Barba, Dave Barmore, Caroline and Ray Bingham, Roger Cain, Alan C. Carey, Ed Davies, Lou Drummond, Derrel Fleener, Rene Francillon, Wayne Gomes, Kevin Grantham, Alan Griffith, Karen B. Haack, John Haire, Ted Holgerson, Dennis Jenkins, Norm Jukes, Bob Kennedy, Robert Kropp, Tillie and William T. Larkins, Dave Leininger, Nate Leong, Peter B. Lewis, Gerry Liang, Michael H. Marlow, Byron May, Shayne Meder, Yvonne and Dale Messimer, Ken Miller, Gina Morello, Dan Morgan, Paul Negri, Robert Nishimura, Dan O'Hara, Michael O'Leary, Terry Panopalis, Donna Pitaro, Teresa Pittman, Peter Rabyk, Taigh Ramey, Ron Sathre, Lee Scales, Doug Scroggins, Phil Smith, Marc Sova, Jim Sullivan, Scott Thompson, Rick Turner, Richard VanderMeulen, Armand and Karen Veronico, Betty Veronico, Tony and Kathleen Veronico, and Randy Walker.